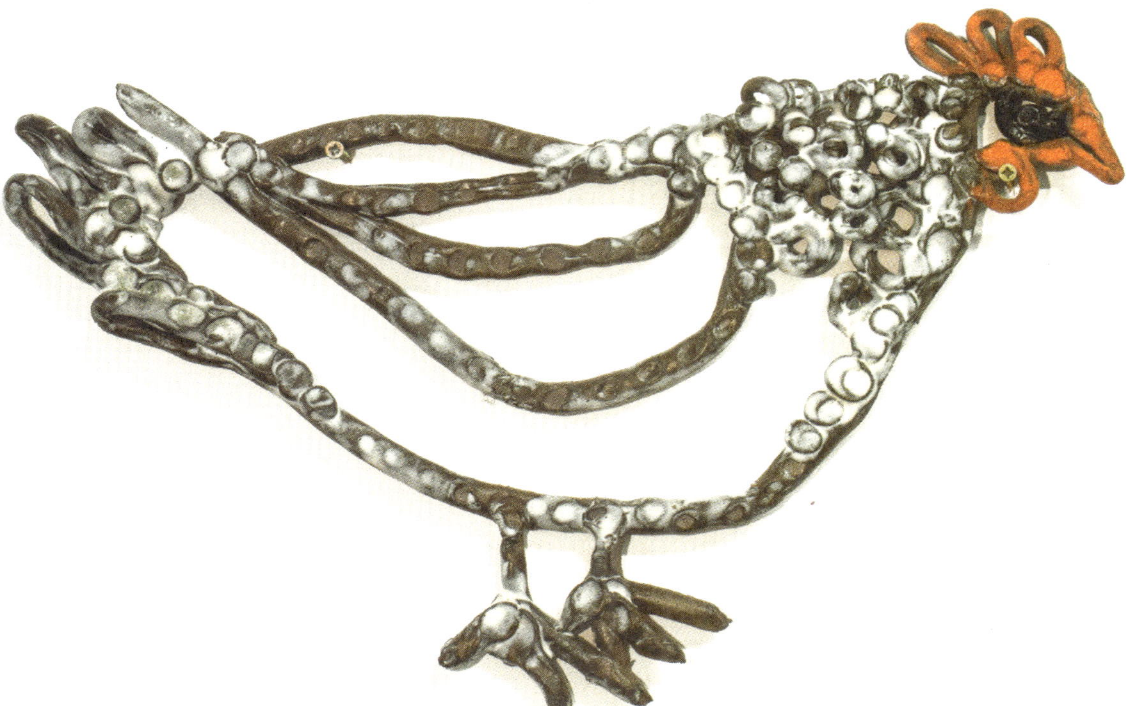

Francesca Anfossi, 2020

AF632016

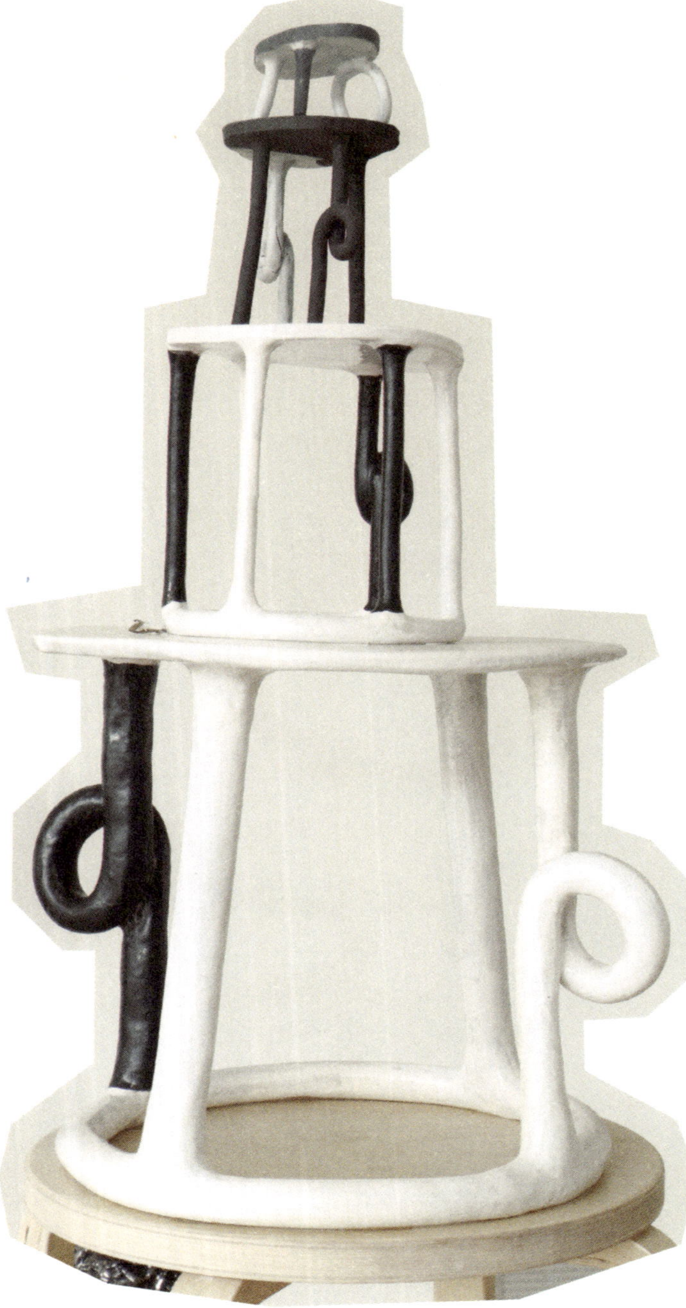

Gerald Mak, 2018

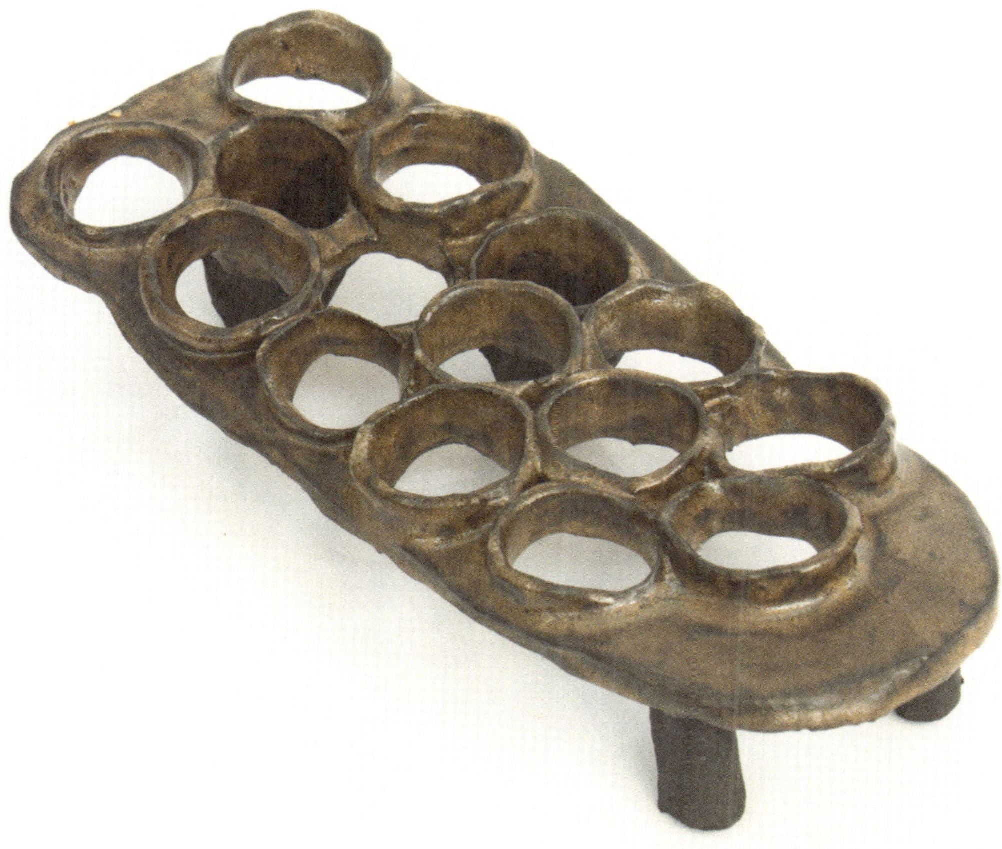

Francesca Anfossi, 2019

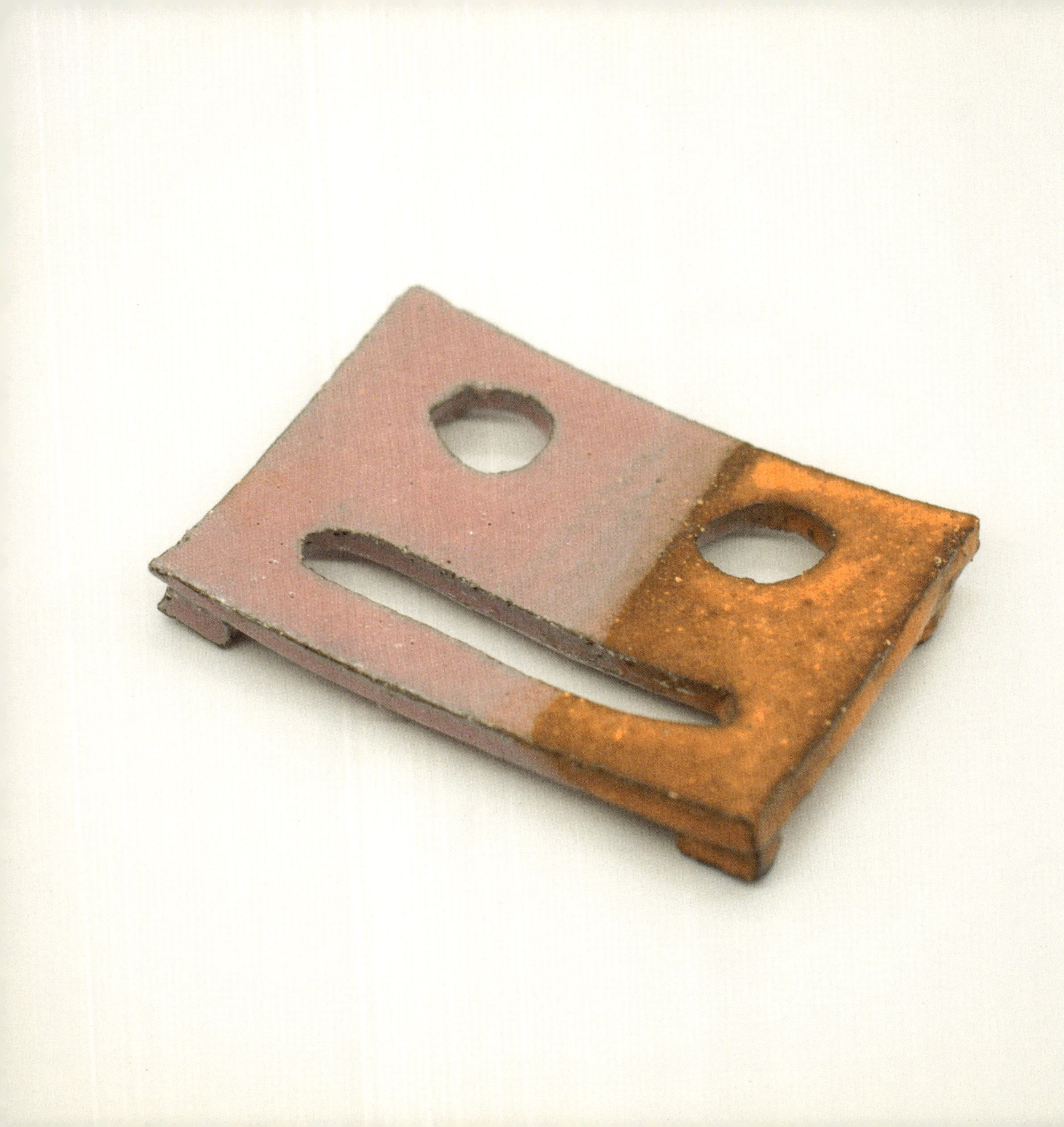

Francesca Anfossi, 2018

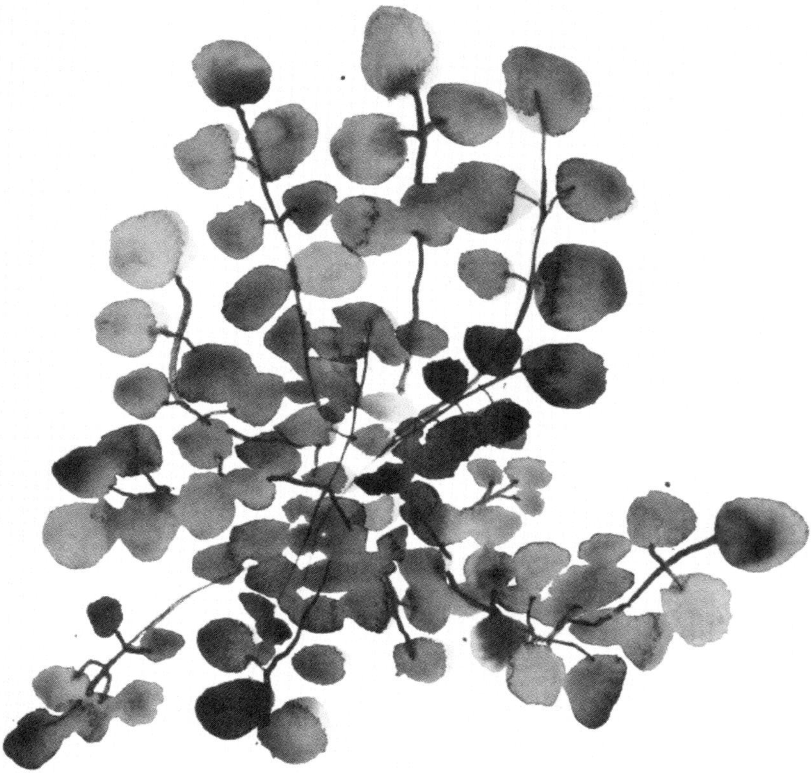

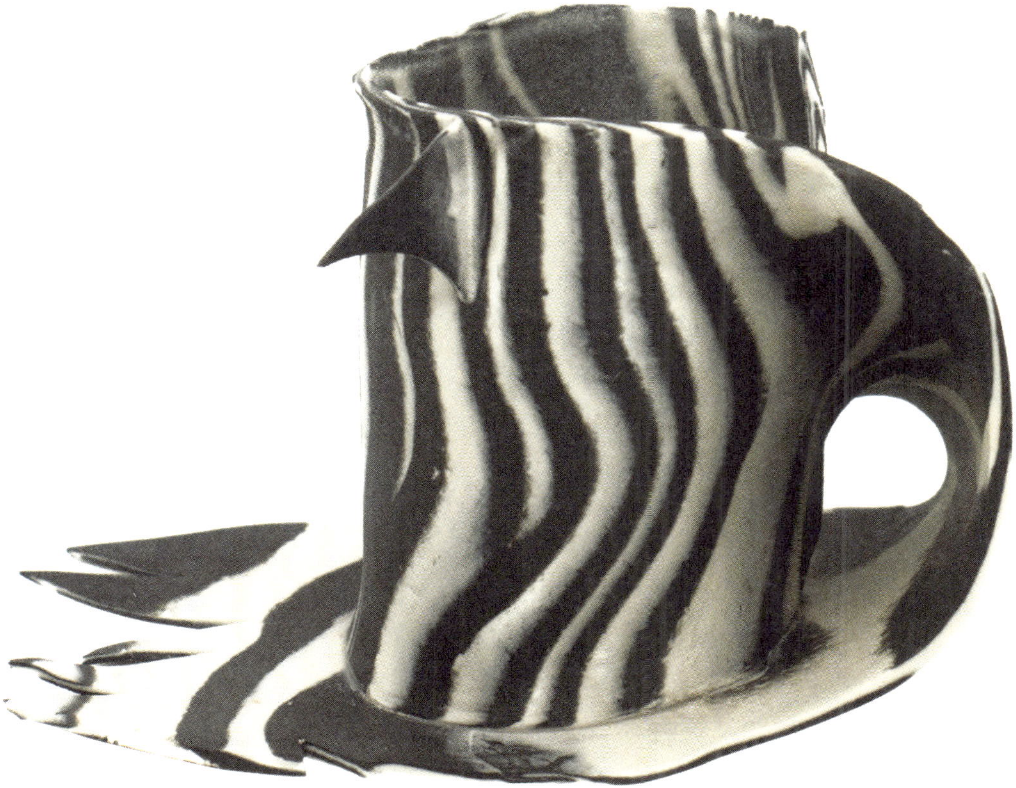

Bea Bonafini, 2019

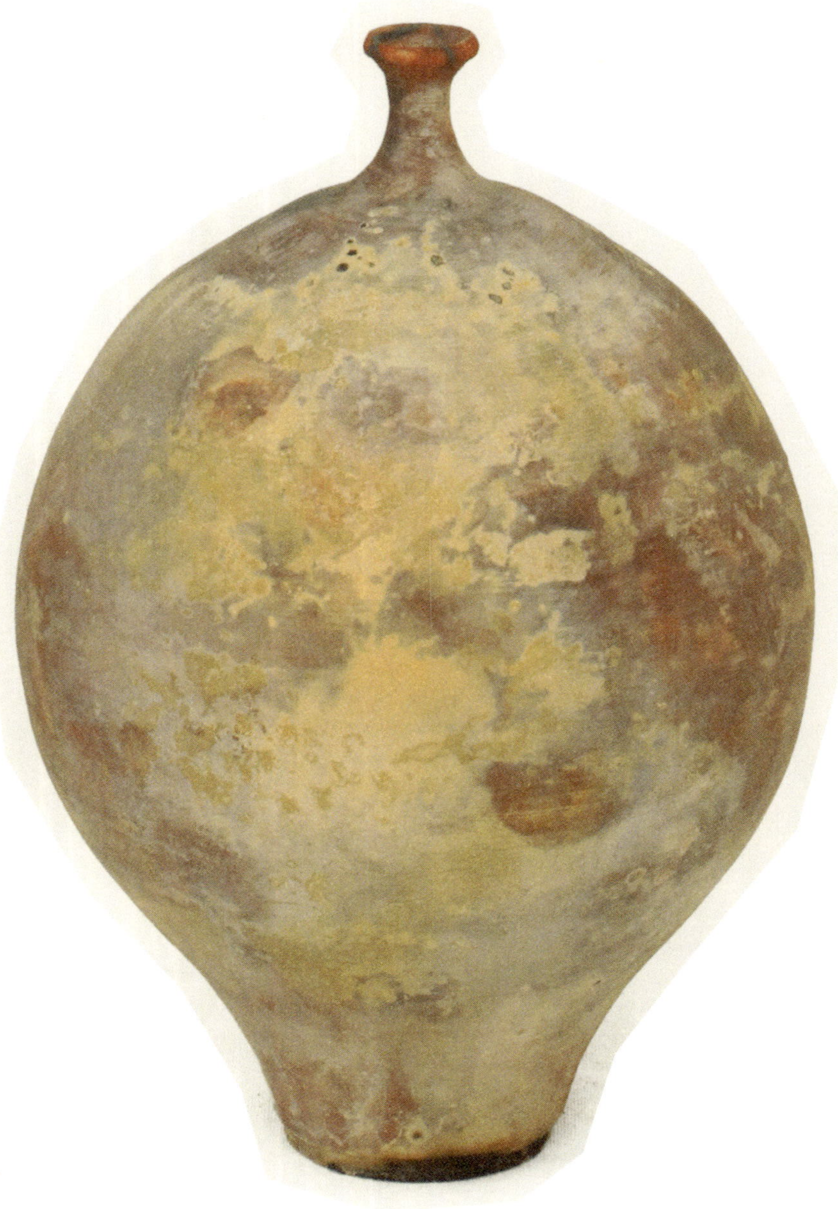

Nam Tran, 2017

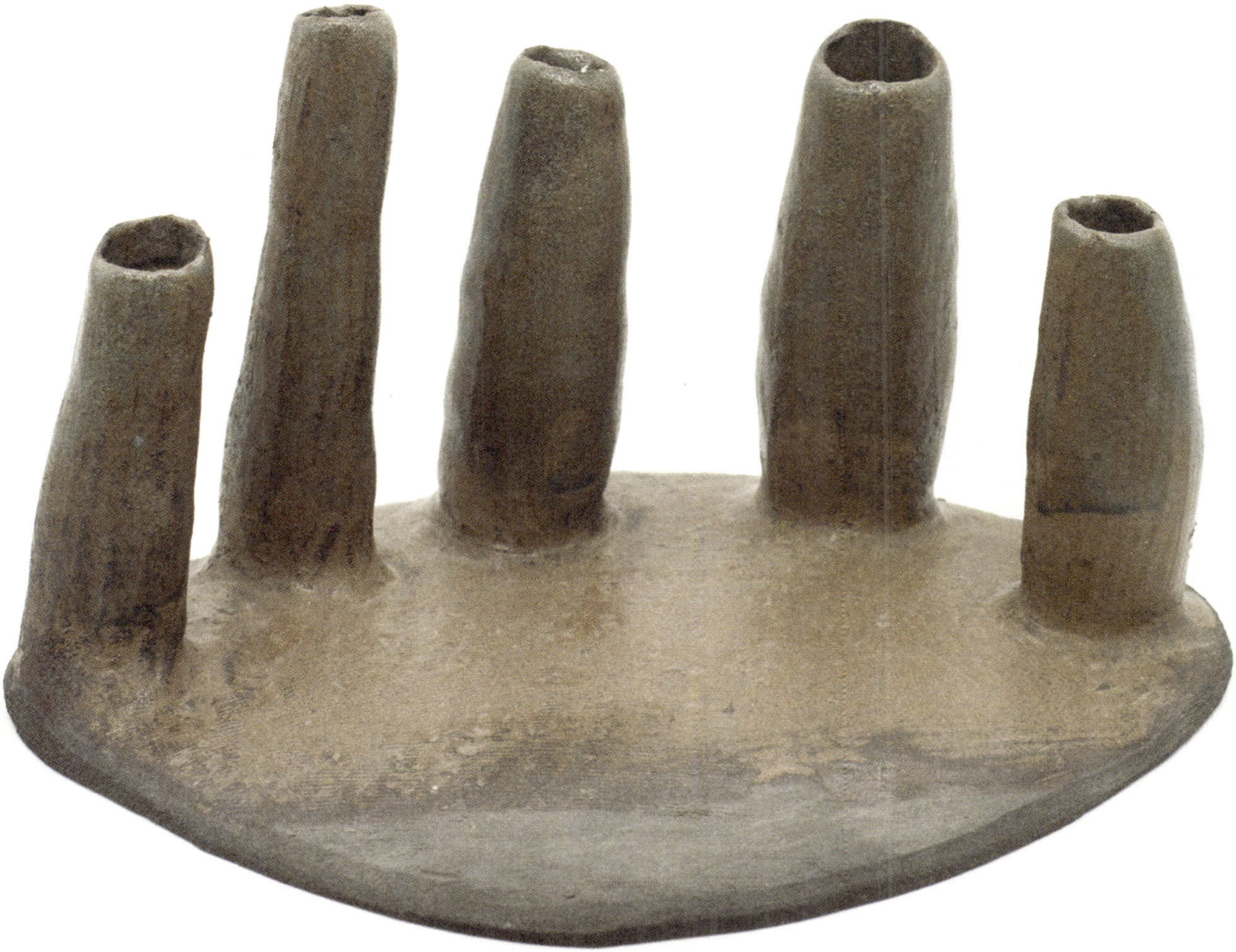

Polly Farquharson, 2019

Foreword
Emily King

I have lived in the neighbourhood around Camden Square for almost thirty years, with a short interlude in West London in the mid-1990s. My deeply grooved mental map of the area began to form soon after university. Employed as a glorified version of a secretary in an arts institution, I shared a house on Marquis Road with a pair of trainee teachers. The best-trod path from our front door was to the almost-always-open shop in the petrol station on Brecknock Road – pints of milk, breakfast cereal and chocolate were our stock in trade. On a healthier note, it was from that house that I first traced the route to the canal at Royal College Street, from where you can run all the way to the Regent's Park without meeting a road. Apart from snack runs and park runs, at that stage our journeys were mainly towards tube stations and bus stops, ways into the wider world.

Returning to the area with small children, a new network emerged. Our family's major back-and-forth was to the nursery and the primary school, and I often found myself on the way to the organic food shops on Brecknock Road. No longer a set of anonymous front doors, the streets were now peppered with the houses of my children's friends, or the dogs we stroked every day and their owners, or bizarre domestic junk yards we watched with fascination (the wood pile at 55 St Augustine's Road was a thing of wonder). During this period, Rochester Square was a blank spot. Initially a wall of plants on the way to my youngest daughter's nursery, it became the source of pungent aromas and the sound of bongo drums opposite my friend Katherine's house. It was obviously a substantial size, but being inaccessible, it did not occupy space in my impression of the neighbourhood.

That changed five years ago. On hearing from a neighbour, Ricky Burdett, that the square had been bought by Francesca Anfossi and Eric Wragge, a local couple with ambitions to create some kind of community arts project, I made contact to arrange a visit. That was back in July 2016; in the time since, Rochester Square has become a significant part of what it means for me to live in Camden Square. Drinking coffee with Francesca for the first time in the then makeshift ceramic studio, I learned about her and Eric's plans. A few months later, I threw my first pot under the guidance of Nam Tran (I enjoyed the experience, but it's not a practice that the world needs me to continue), and a little while after that I joined the original communal dinner.

Sitting at the common table in the studio, I have met many a long-term neighbour for the first time, and it was at Rochester Square that I first ate the bread of the area's brilliant new baker, Andy Strang of Brecknock Road's Bread by Bike. I have introduced close friends to the studio who have gone on to make it their creative home, and my house now holds a light sprinkling of ceramics that started life in the Rochester Square kilns. The space is now firmly integrated into my scheme of the area, yet it still has the potential to be otherworldly. I am thinking in particular of a night when Eric and Francesca fired up the pizza oven (the first iteration of the oven, like the houses in the area, was built from the local clay) to allow my husband to test his latest attempt at dough. We ate pizzas with deliciously charred bases (strictly speaking, we should have sprinkled more water on the paddle) and put the world to rights late into the night. Deep in the garden, lit only by the fire in the oven, the world fell away. Stumbling out of the square into the light

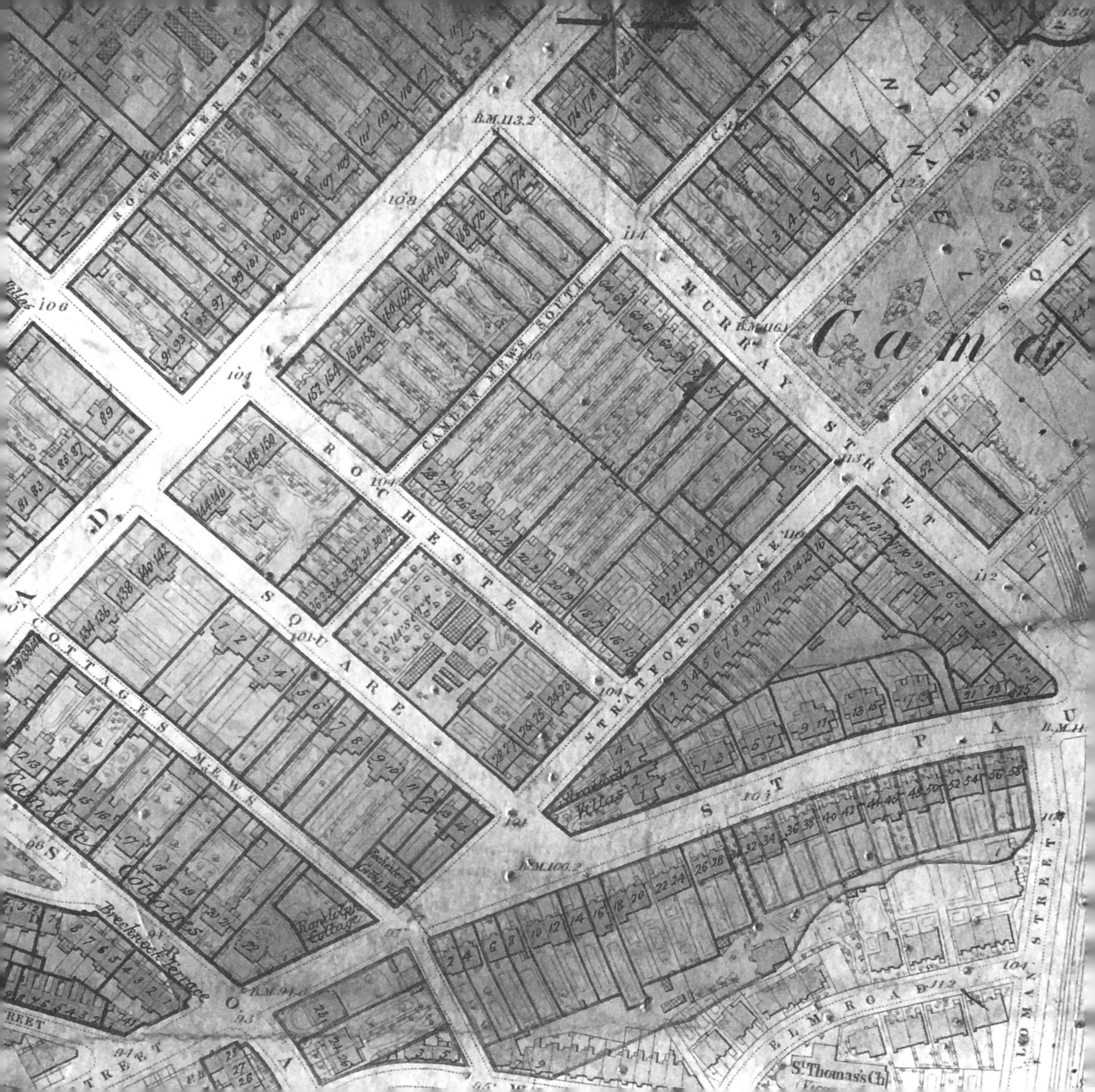
ROCHESTER MEWS
CAMDEN MEWS SOUTH
MURRAY STREET
ROCHESTER
SQUARE
STRATFORD PLACE
COTTAGES MEWS
Nursery
Stratford Villas
Randolph Cottage
Brecknock Terrace
Camden Cottages
ELM ROAD
St Thomas's Ch
Camd

of the streetlamps felt a bit like coming back through the cupboard door in *The Lion, the Witch and the Wardrobe* – a disconcerting reacquaintance with normalcy.

This magical combination of the square being a part of the area while also existing in its own dimension seems perfectly in keeping with its purpose as stipulated in the 1931 London Squares Preservation Act. Rochester Square is one of 461 enclosures specified by the act, which determines that these parcels of land can be used only for 'play, rest or recreation.' It continues, 'The existence of the said squares gardens and enclosures is of great benefit [. . .] by reason of the amenities arising thereby to the inhabitants thereof and by reason of the advantages to health which are thereby afforded.' At the time of the legislation, Rochester Square was being used as a nursery, a function it had had since the 1820s and would have until the 1980s. Francesca and Eric have applied themselves to the garden with the aim of nurturing both edible and ornamental plants. They have instigated a monthly volunteer gardening session, and the participants are rewarded with pizza. It's a very twenty-first-century arrangement, but the health benefits are perfectly in line with the ambitions of 1931. The place is a tonic.

At the risk of sounding hyperbolic, over the last five years my locale has been expanded by Francesca and Eric's activities at Rochester Square. Not only did it become a feature of my mental map, it also functions as a place for connecting with people and ventures. This book stands as a record of all that has gone on in the past as well as a manifesto for the future. Clay, food and garden: I look forward to watching the three intertwined strands of the project bear fruit in the years to come.

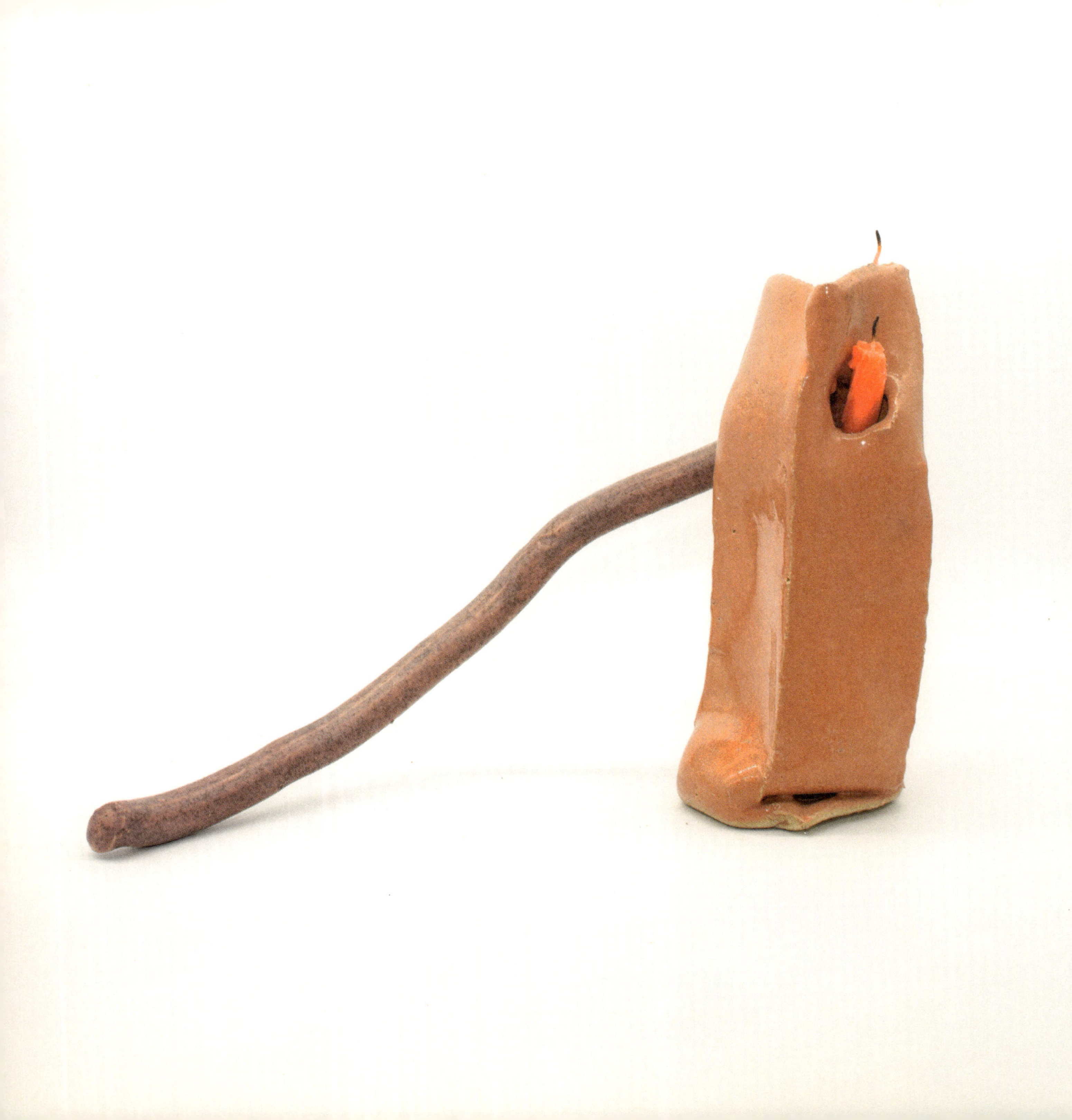

Leigh Johnson, 2019

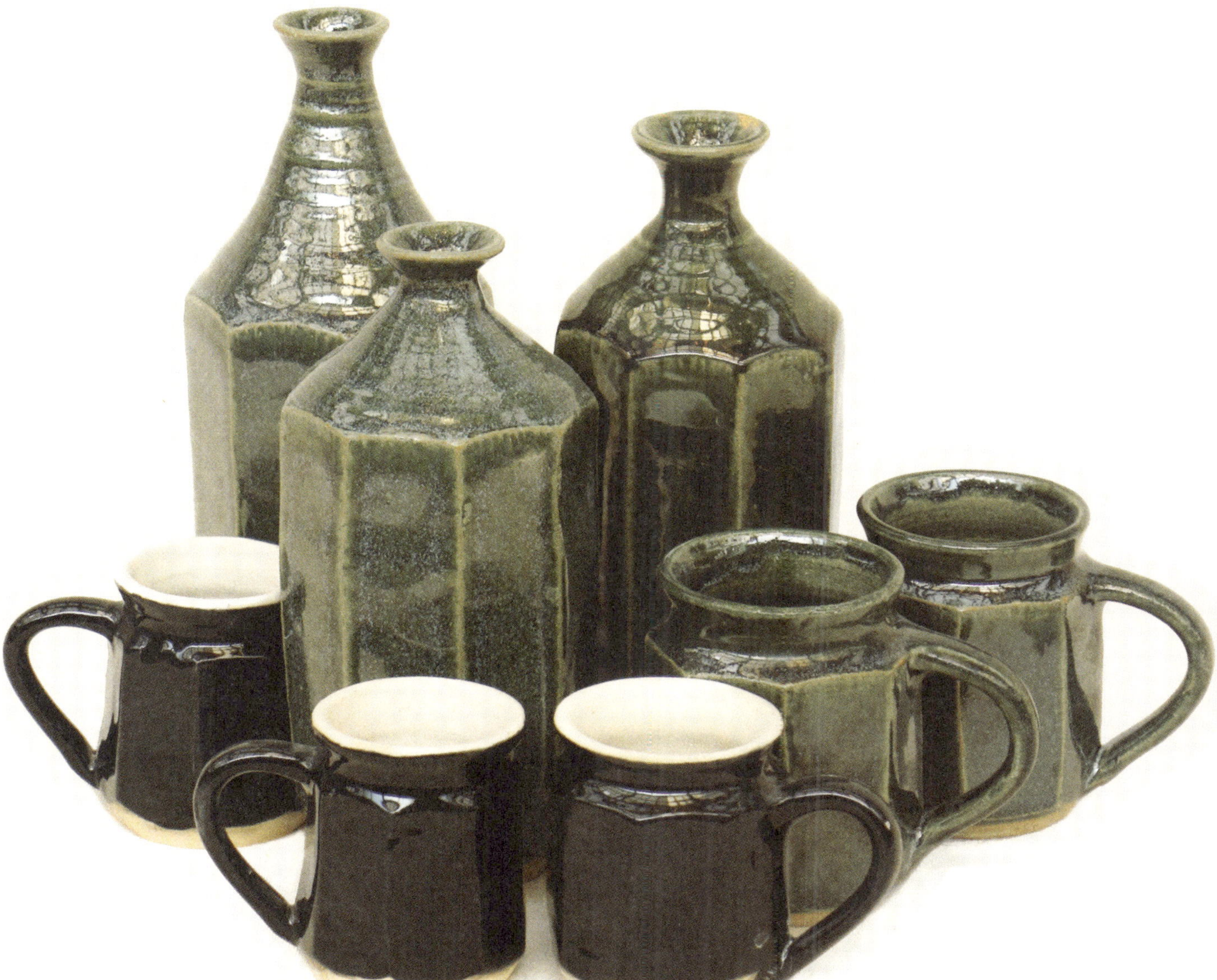

Robert Harbord, 2018

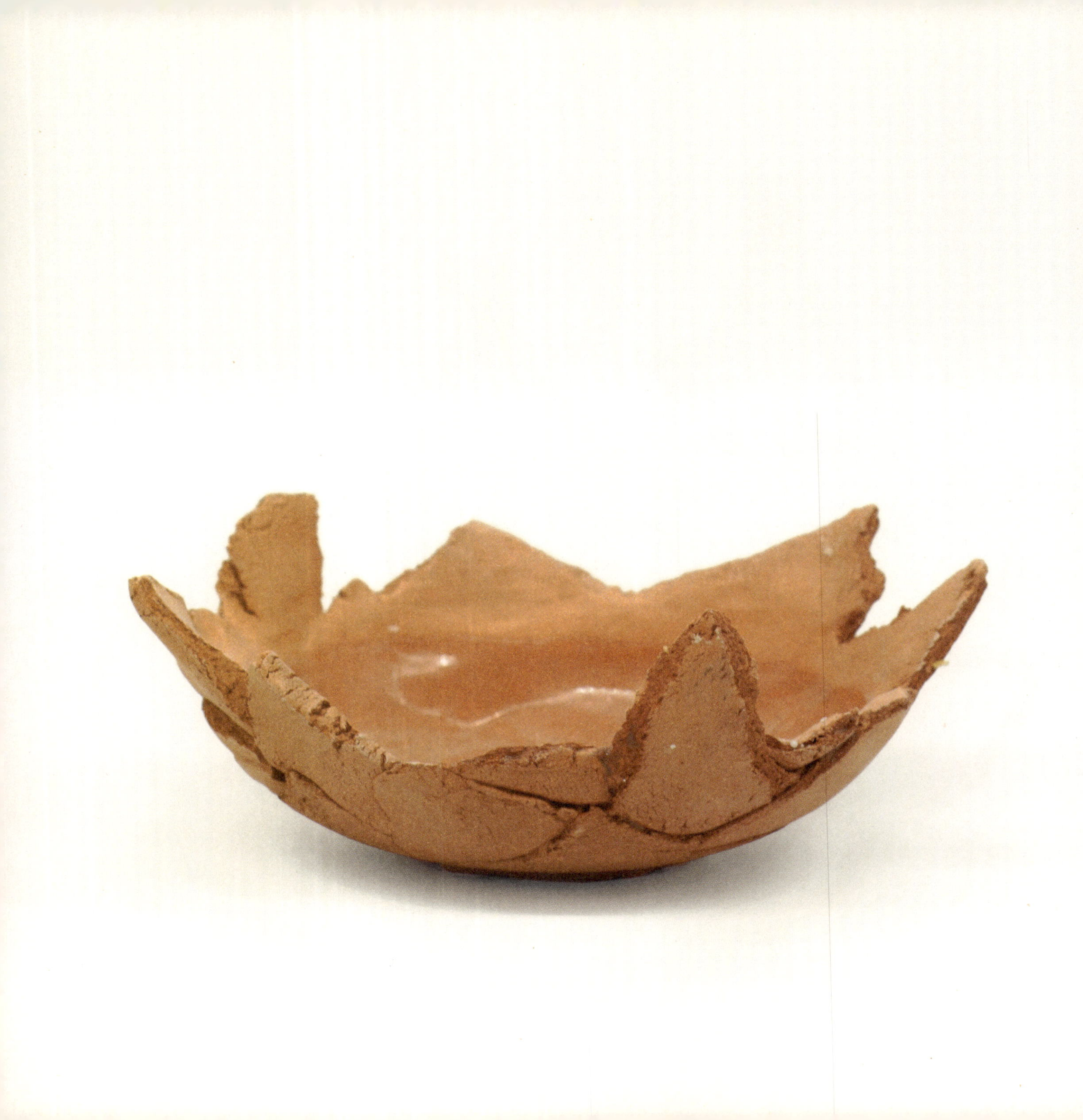

Gerald Mak, Marta Fernàndez and Yoojin Lee, 2019

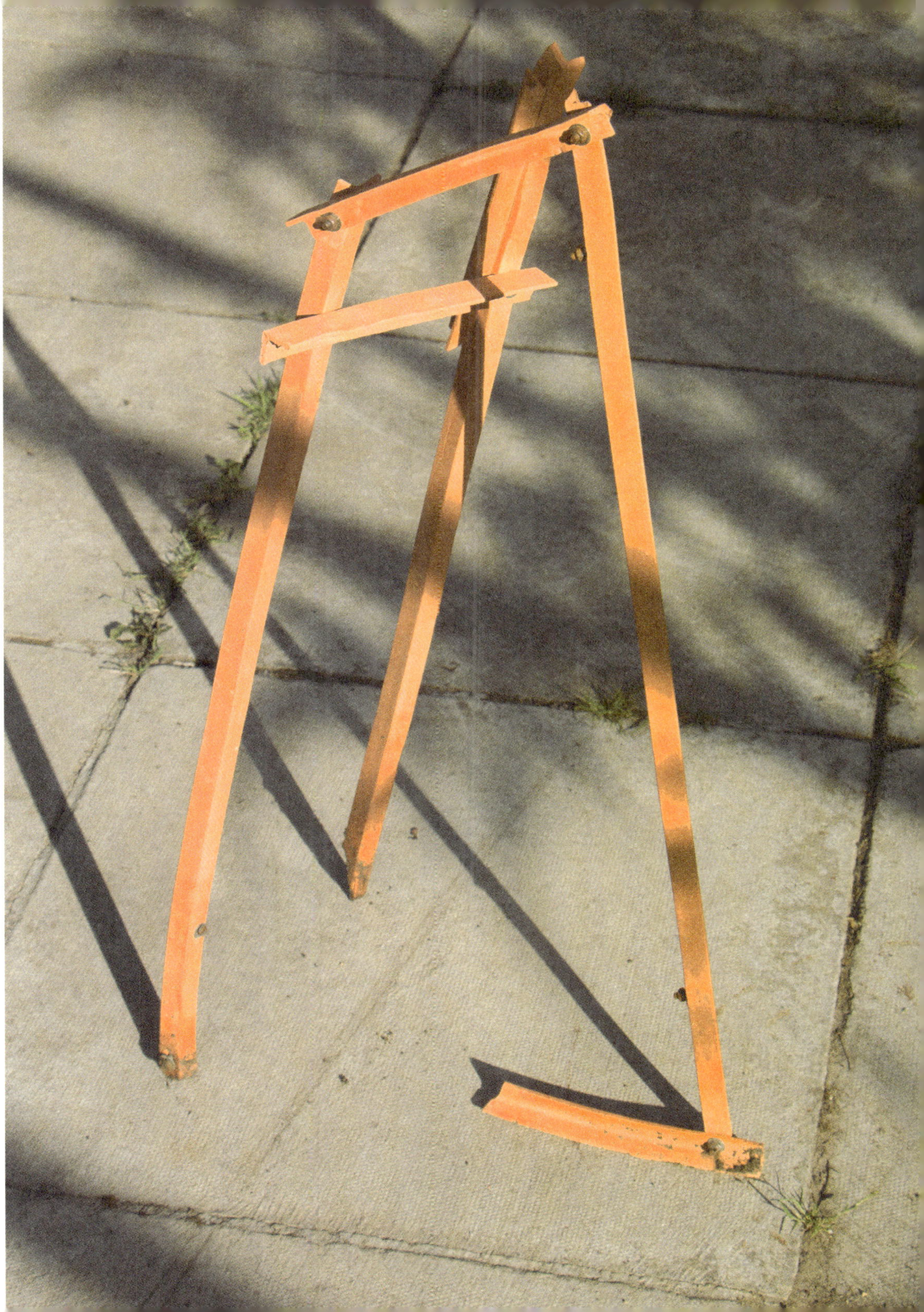

Ryan Orme, 2019

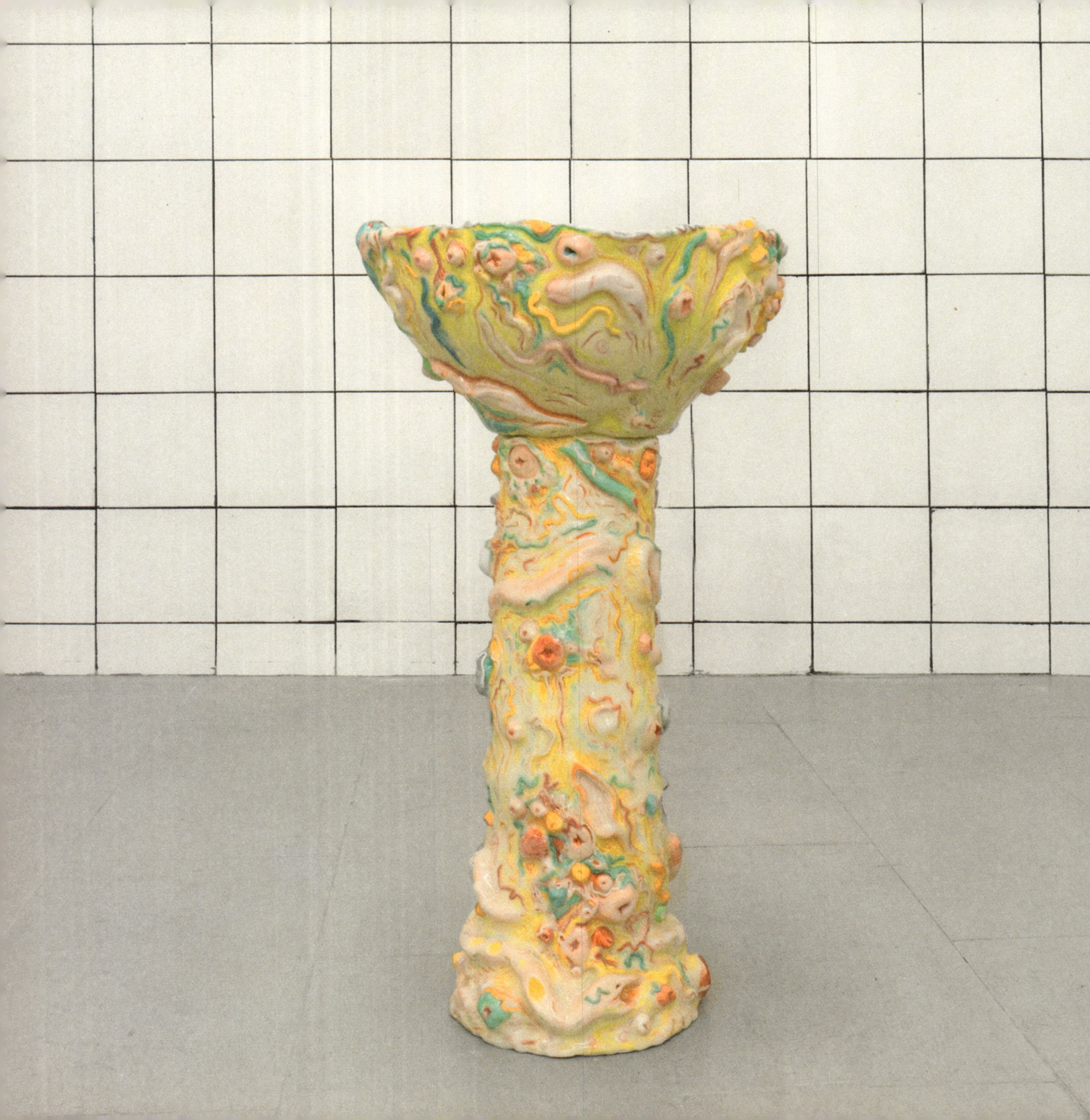

Zoe Williams, 2017

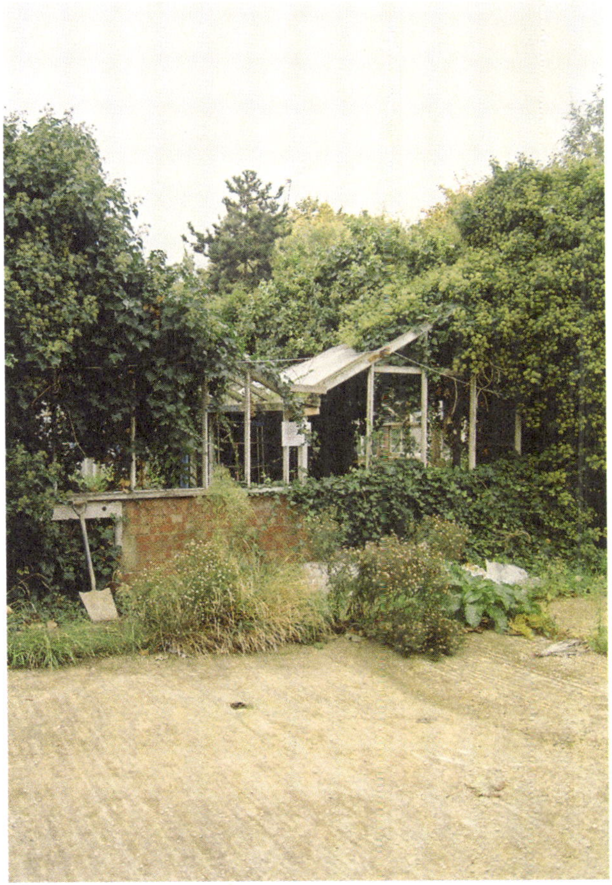

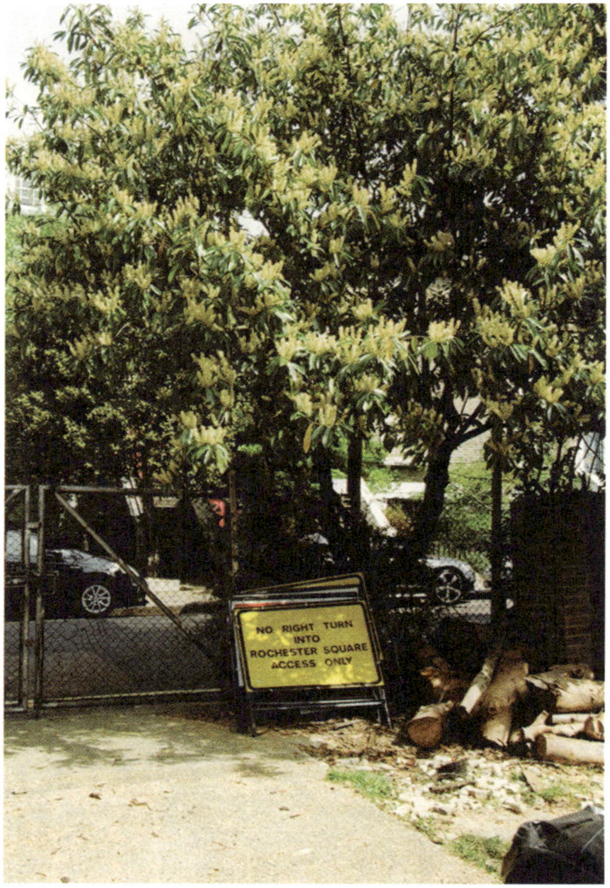
NO RIGHT TURN
INTO
ROCHESTER SQUARE
ACCESS ONLY

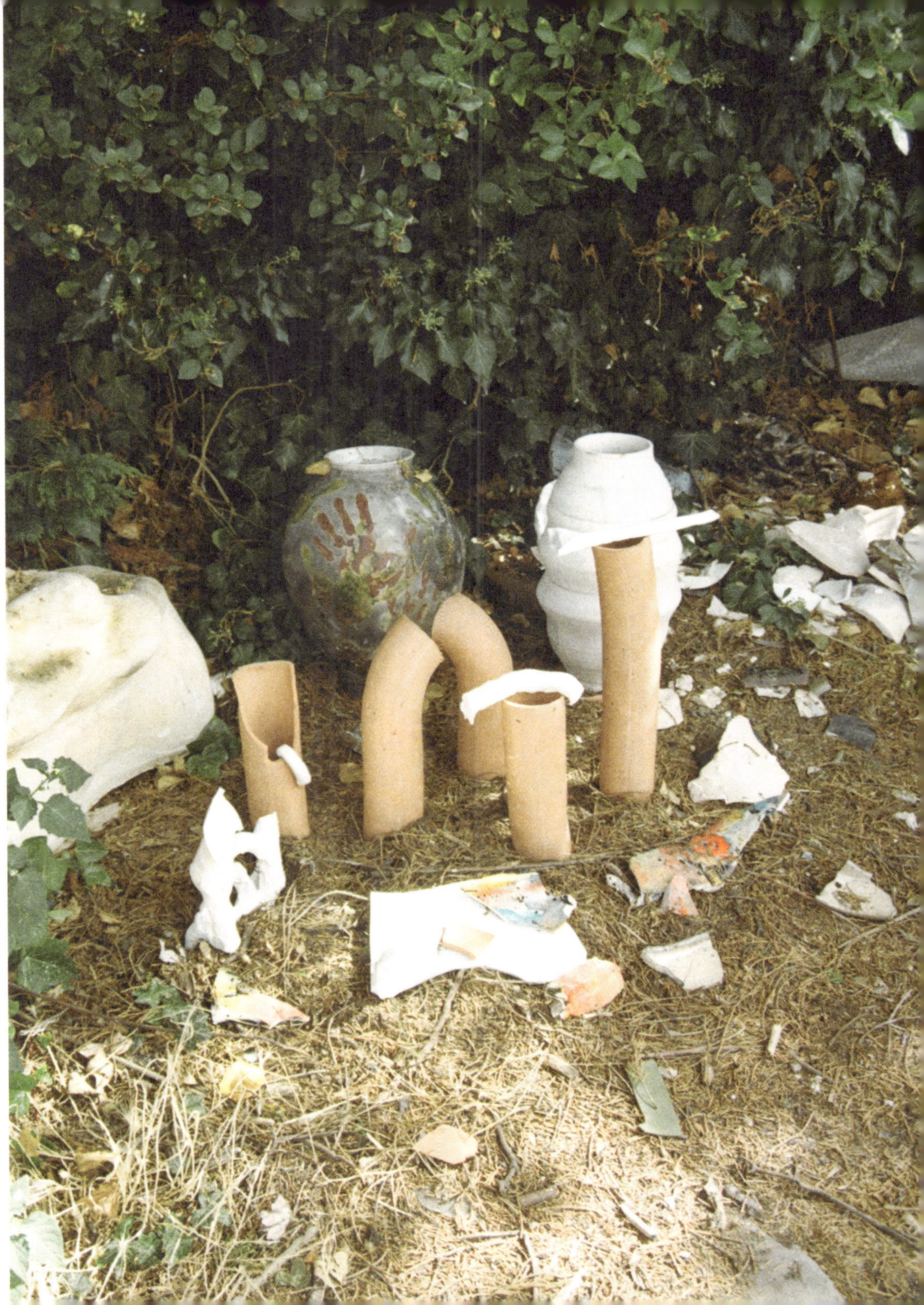

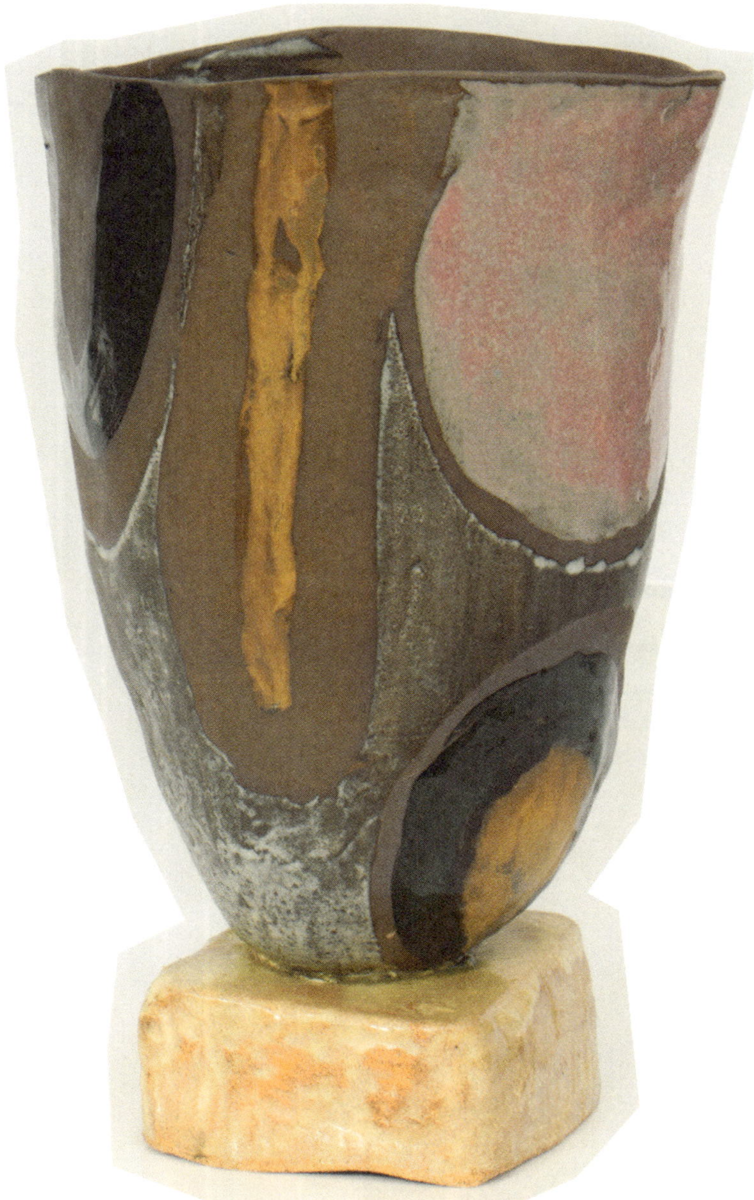

Francesca Anfossi, 2019

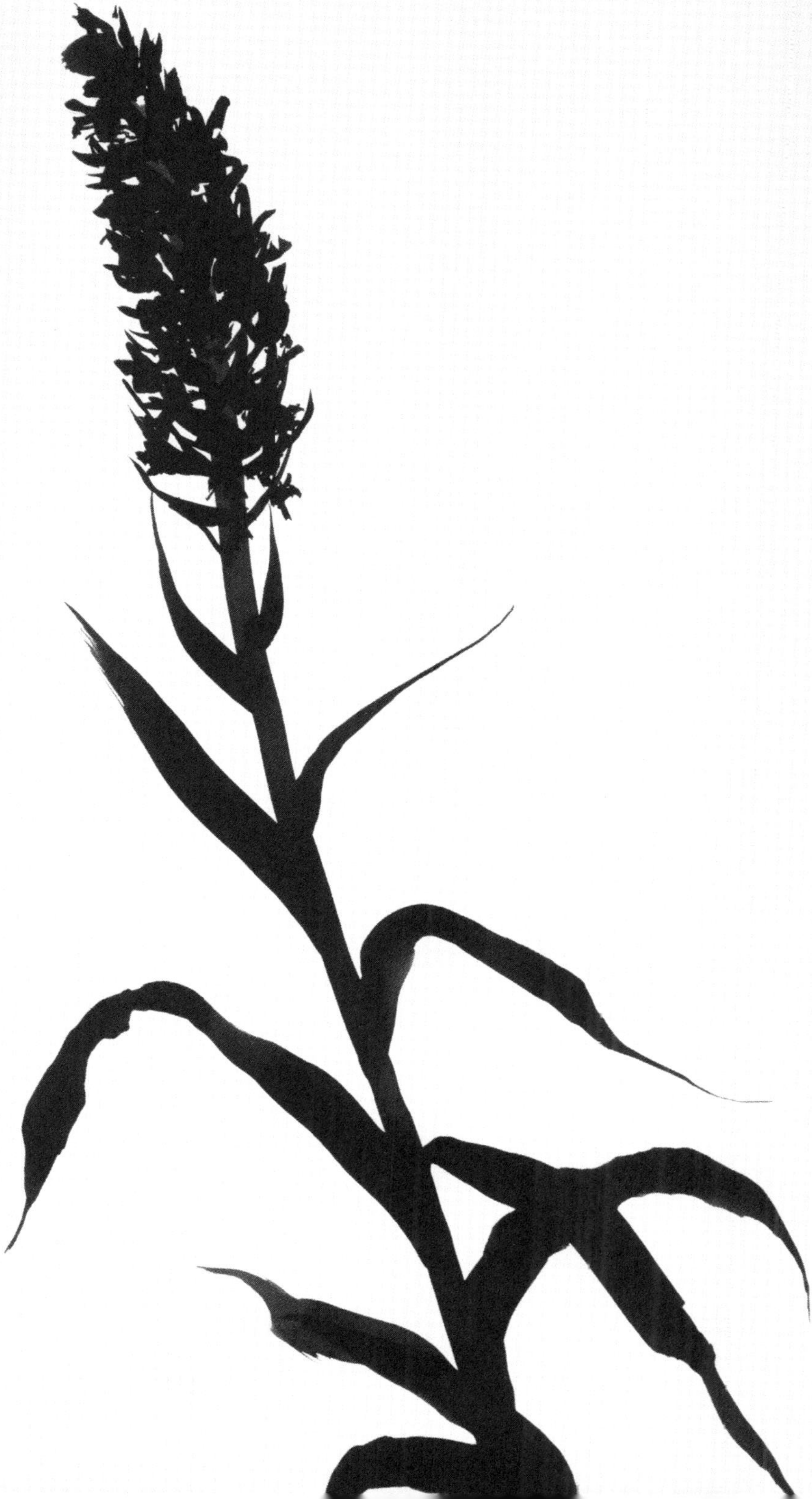

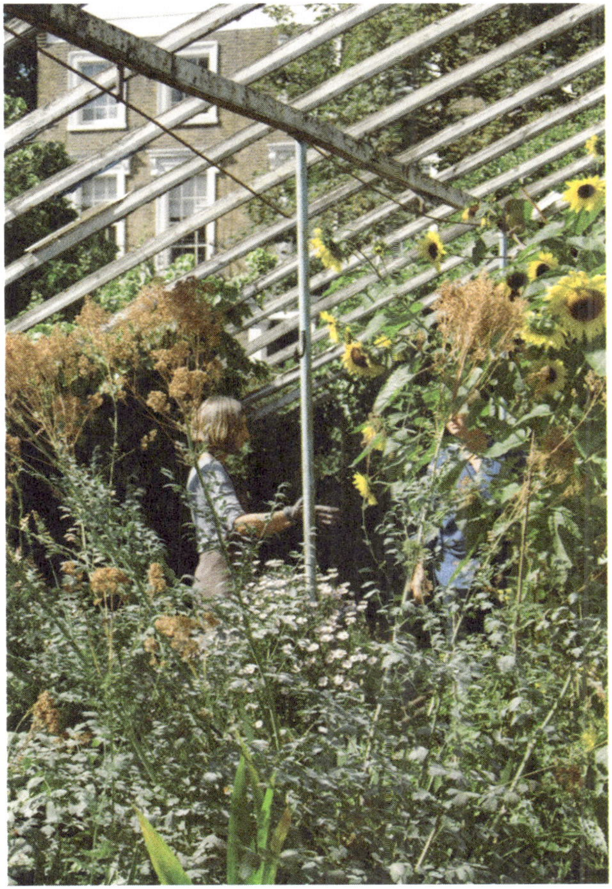

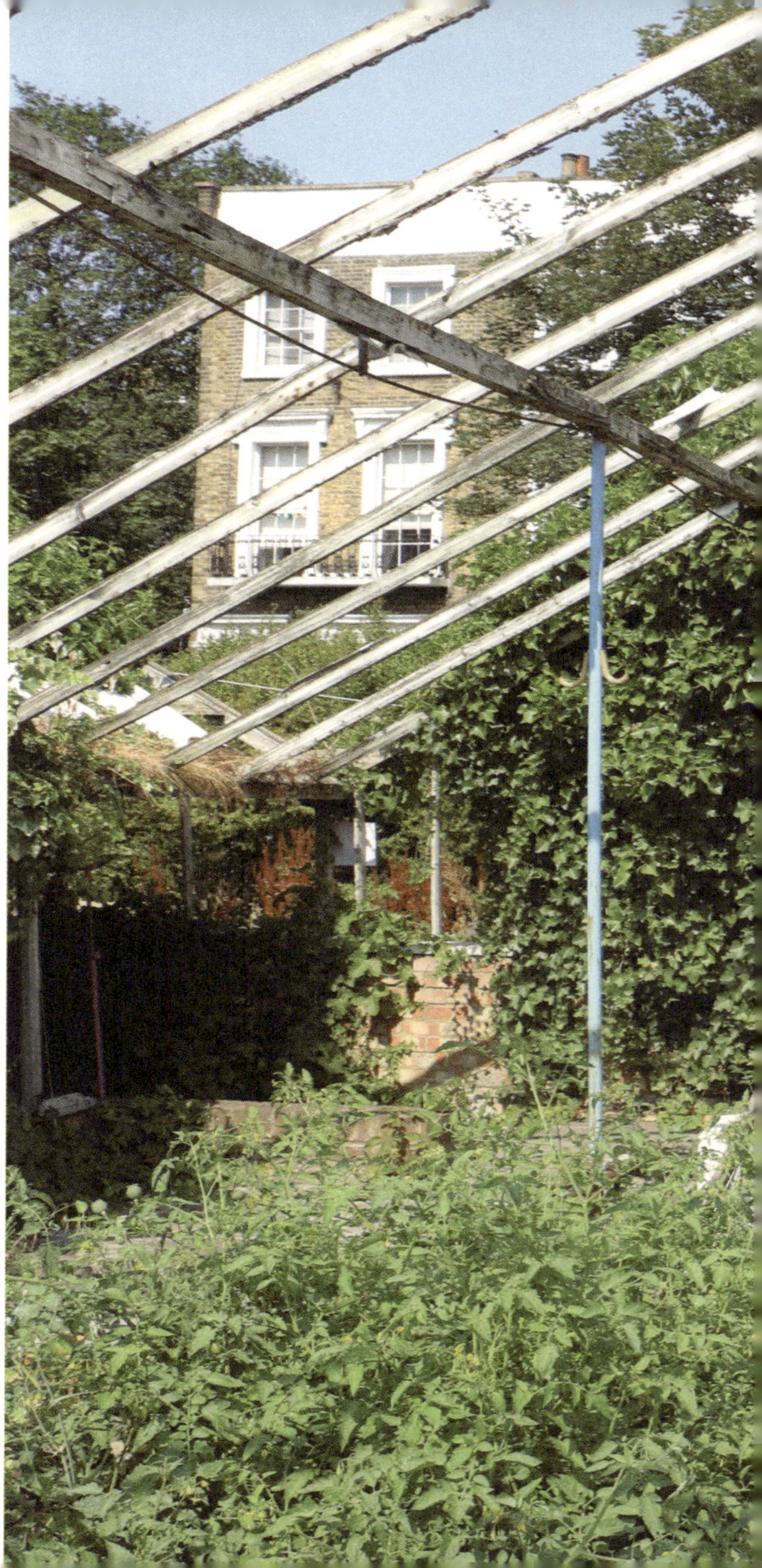

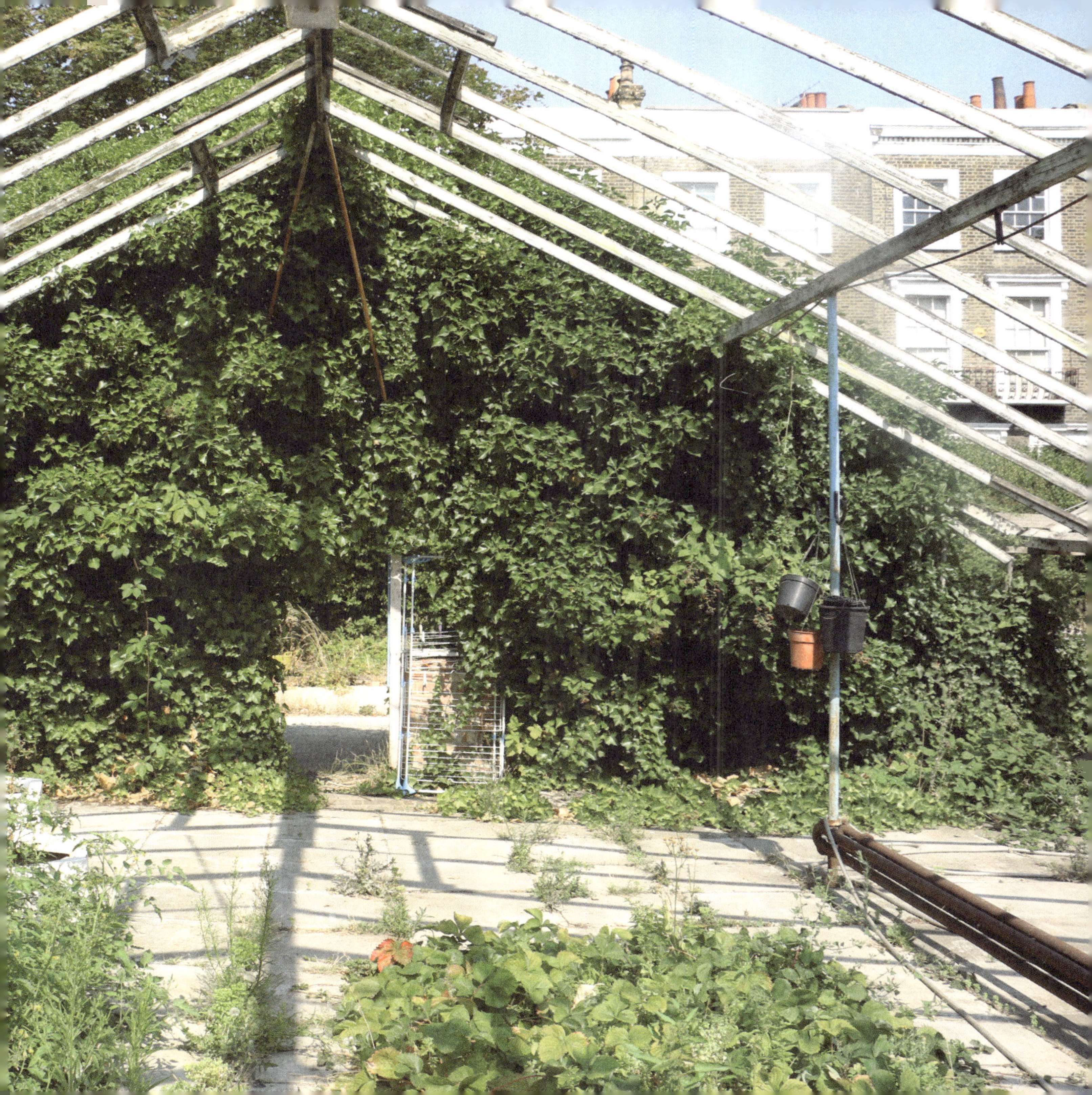

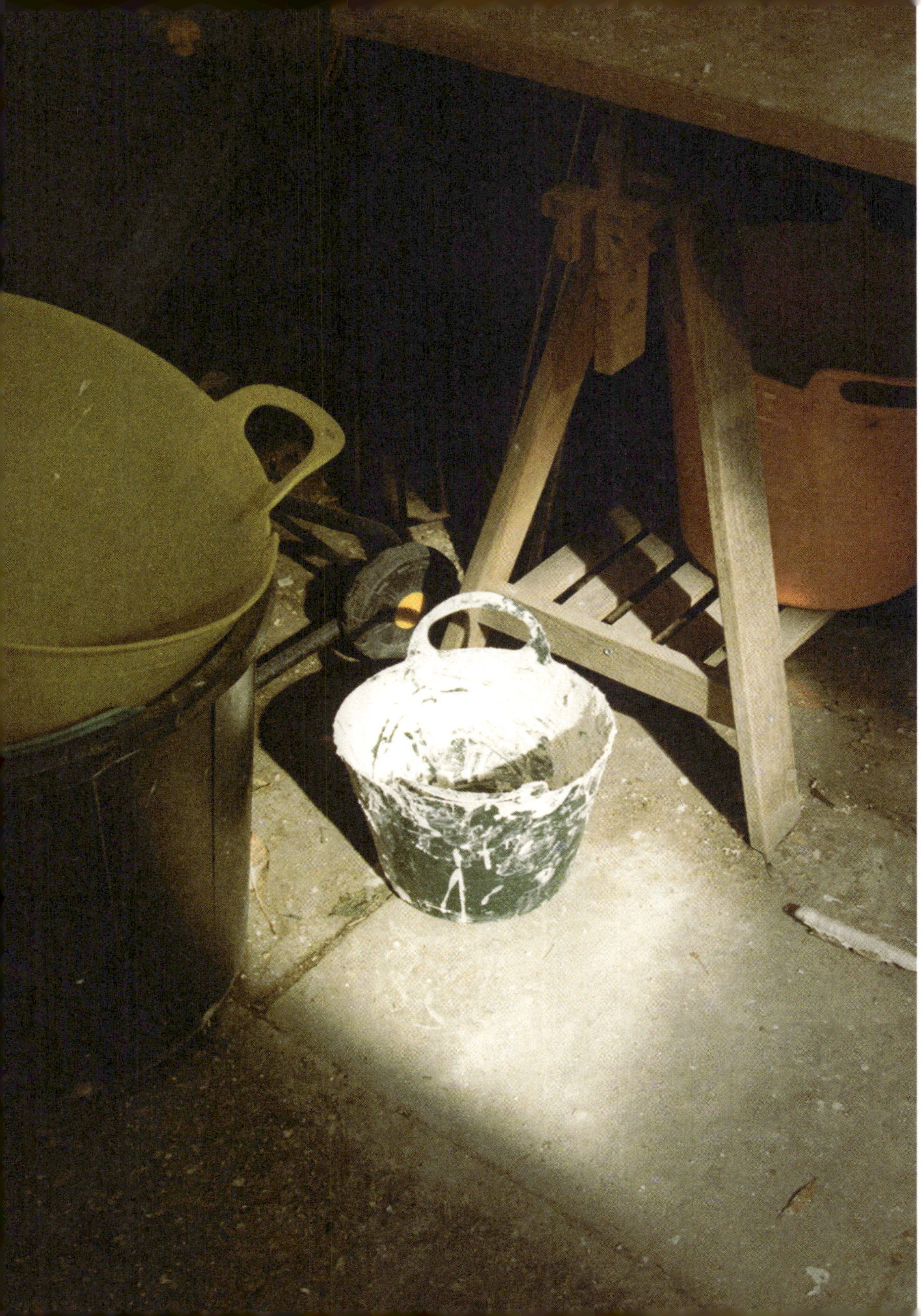

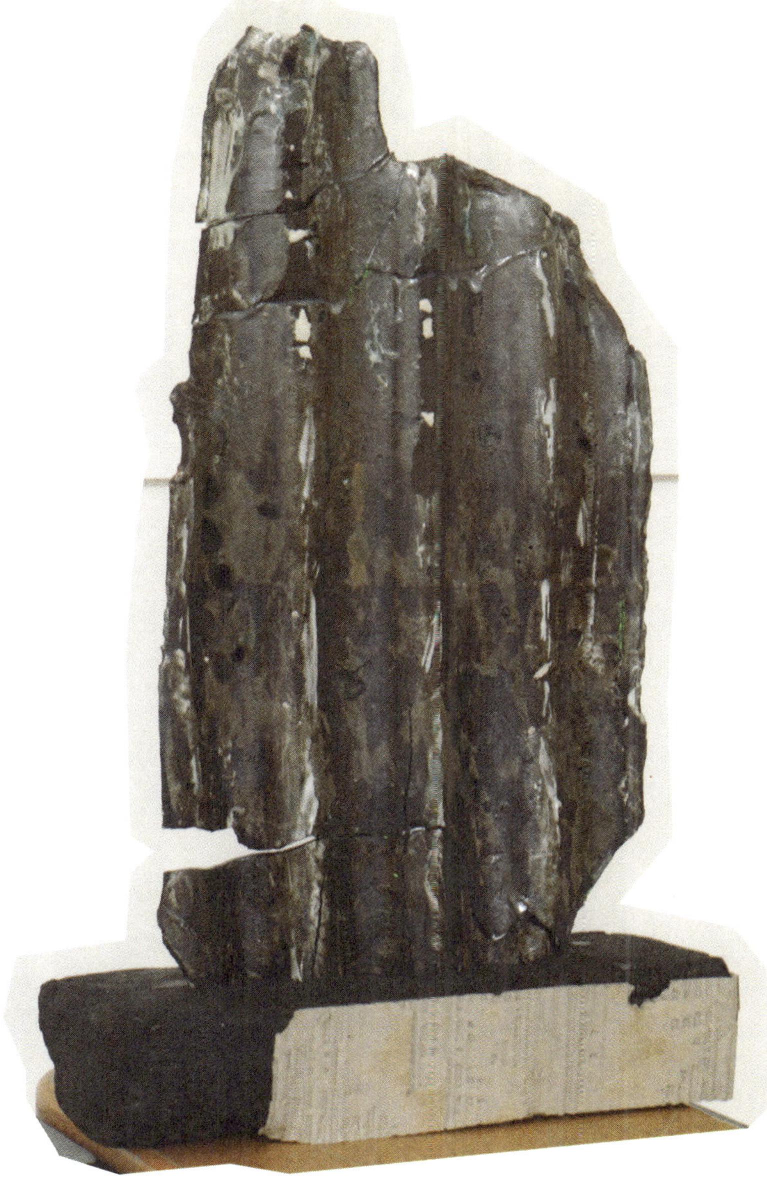

Leviathen Hendricks, 2018

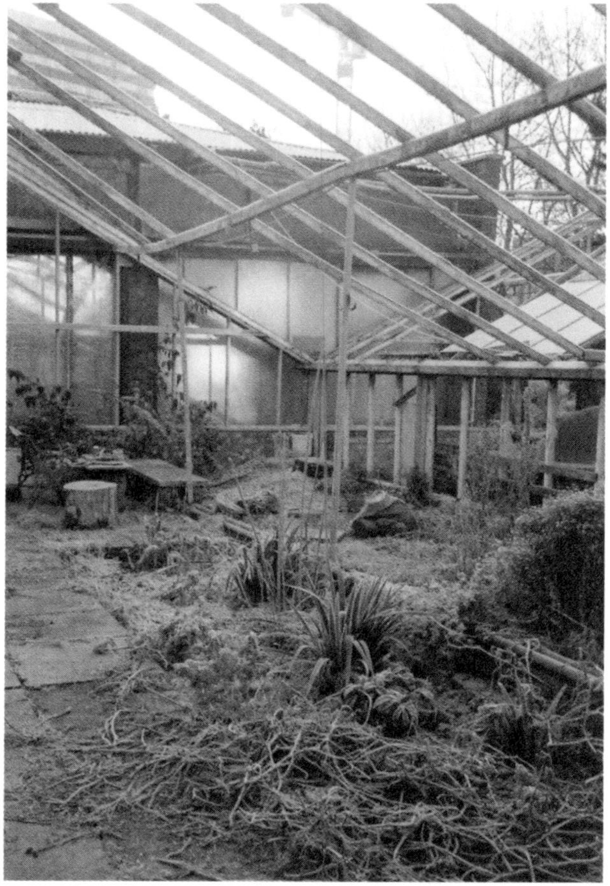

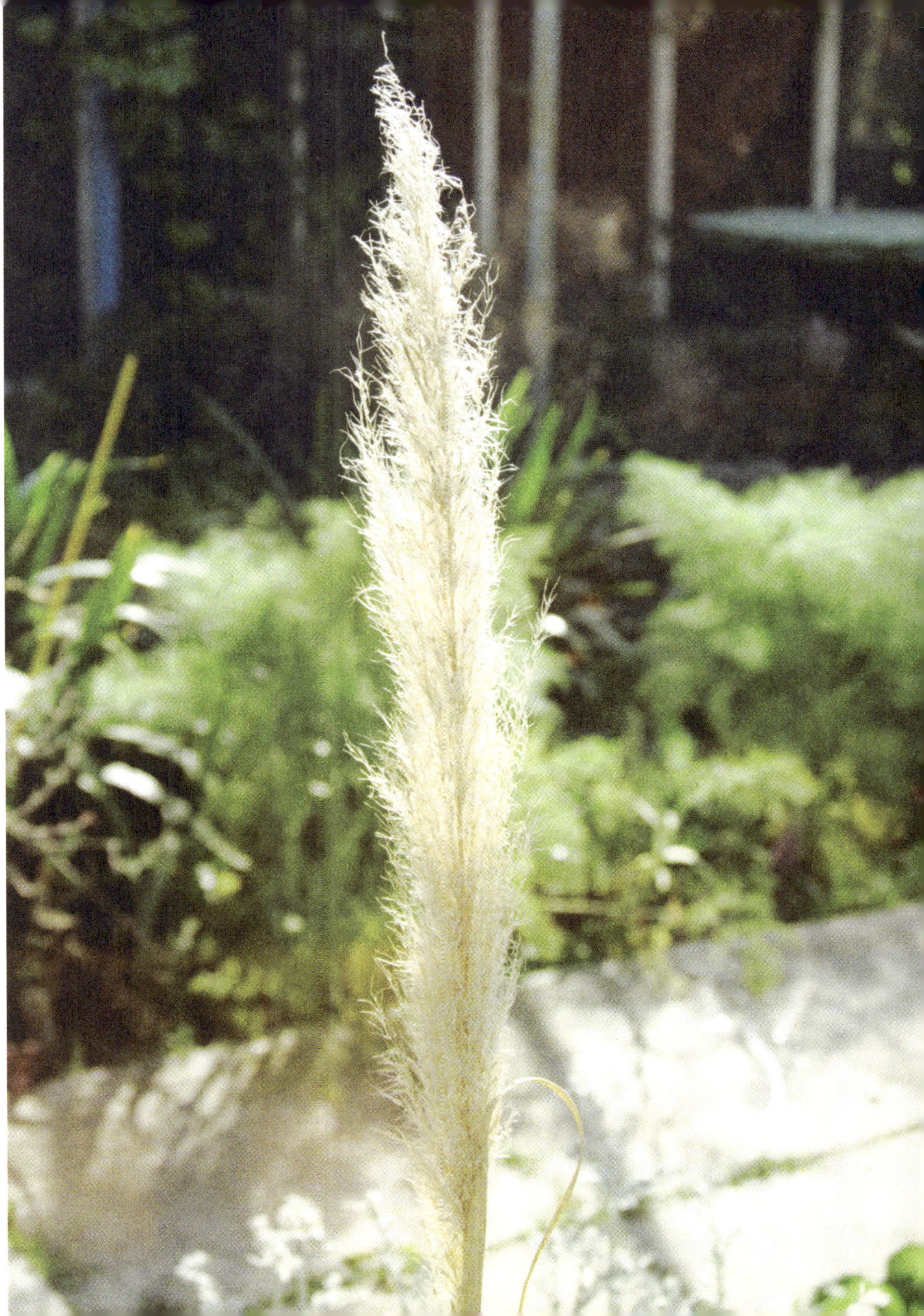

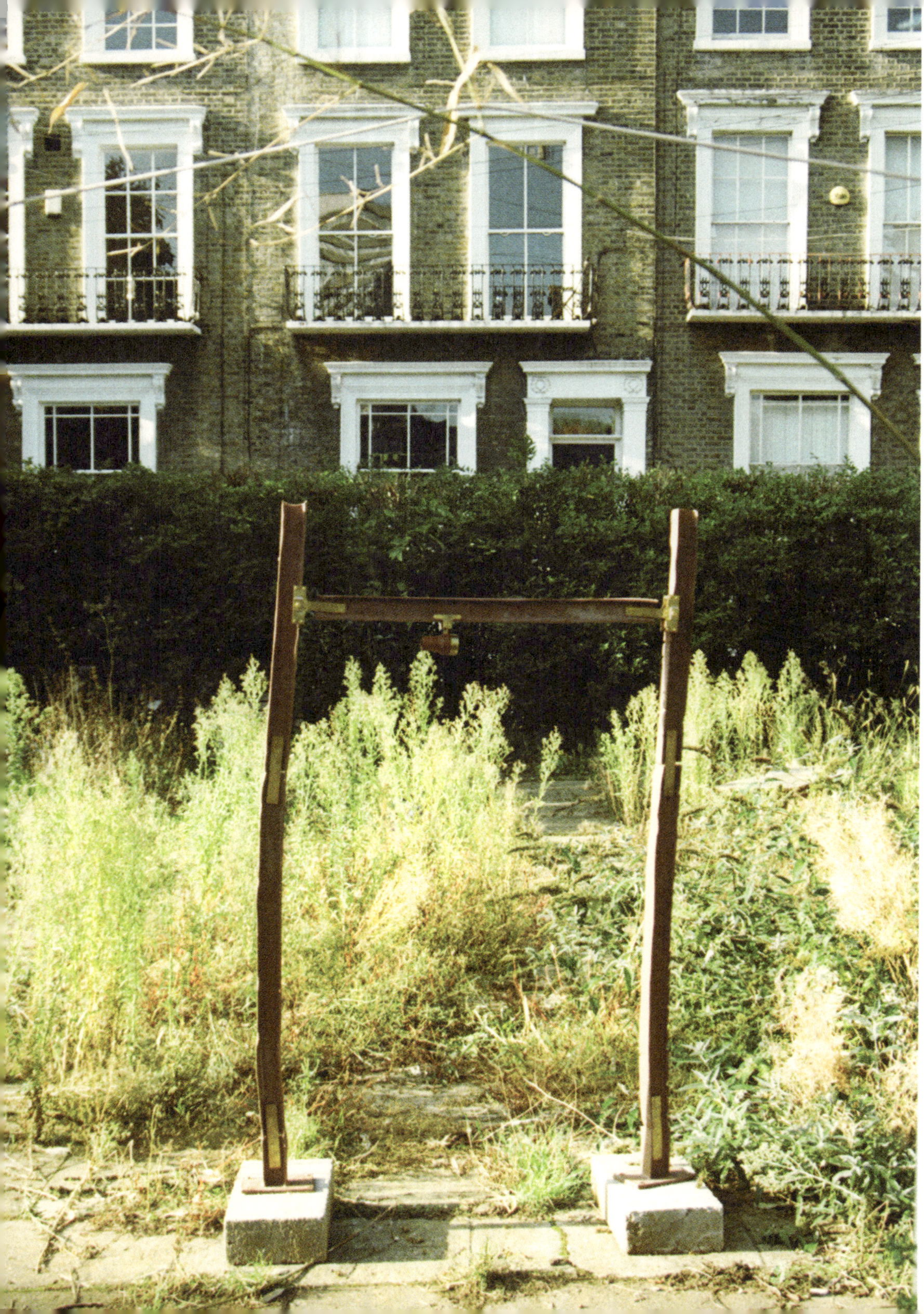

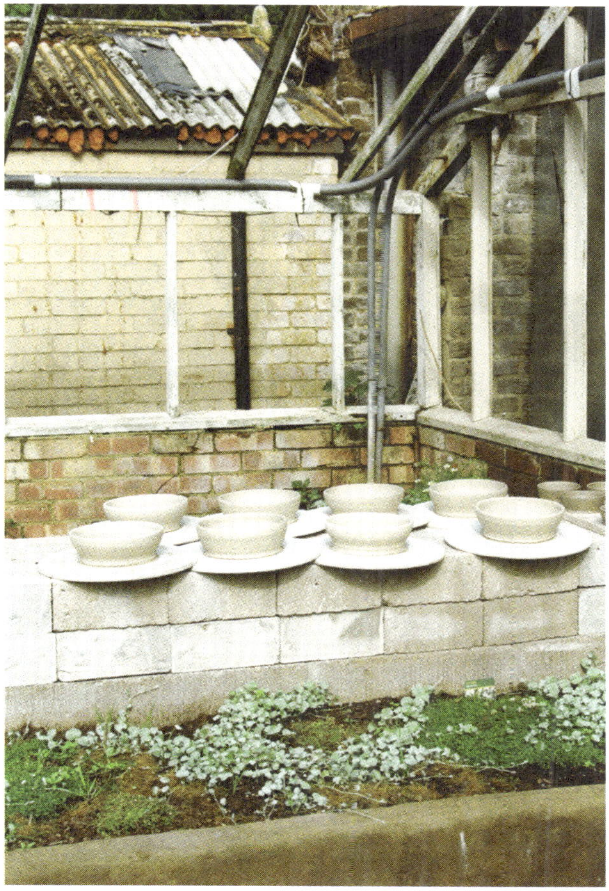

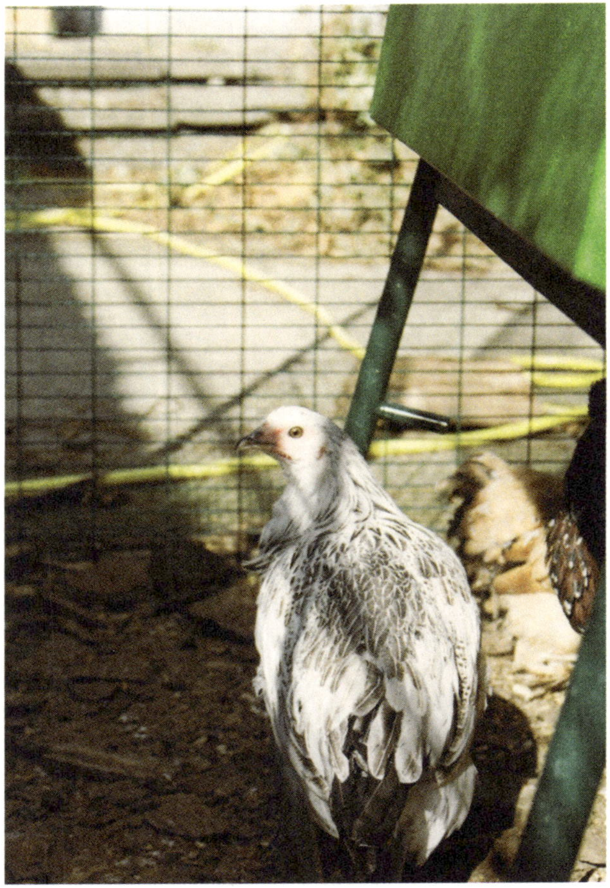

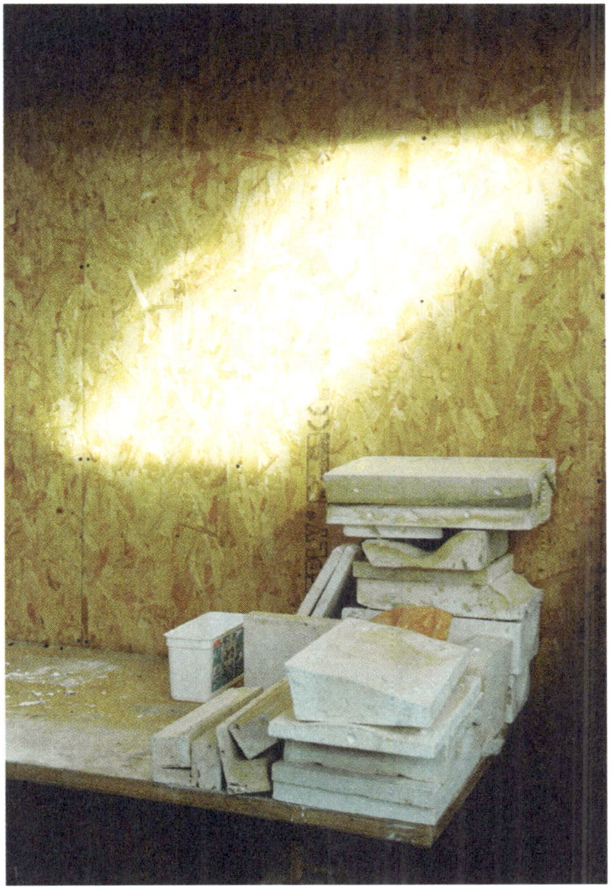

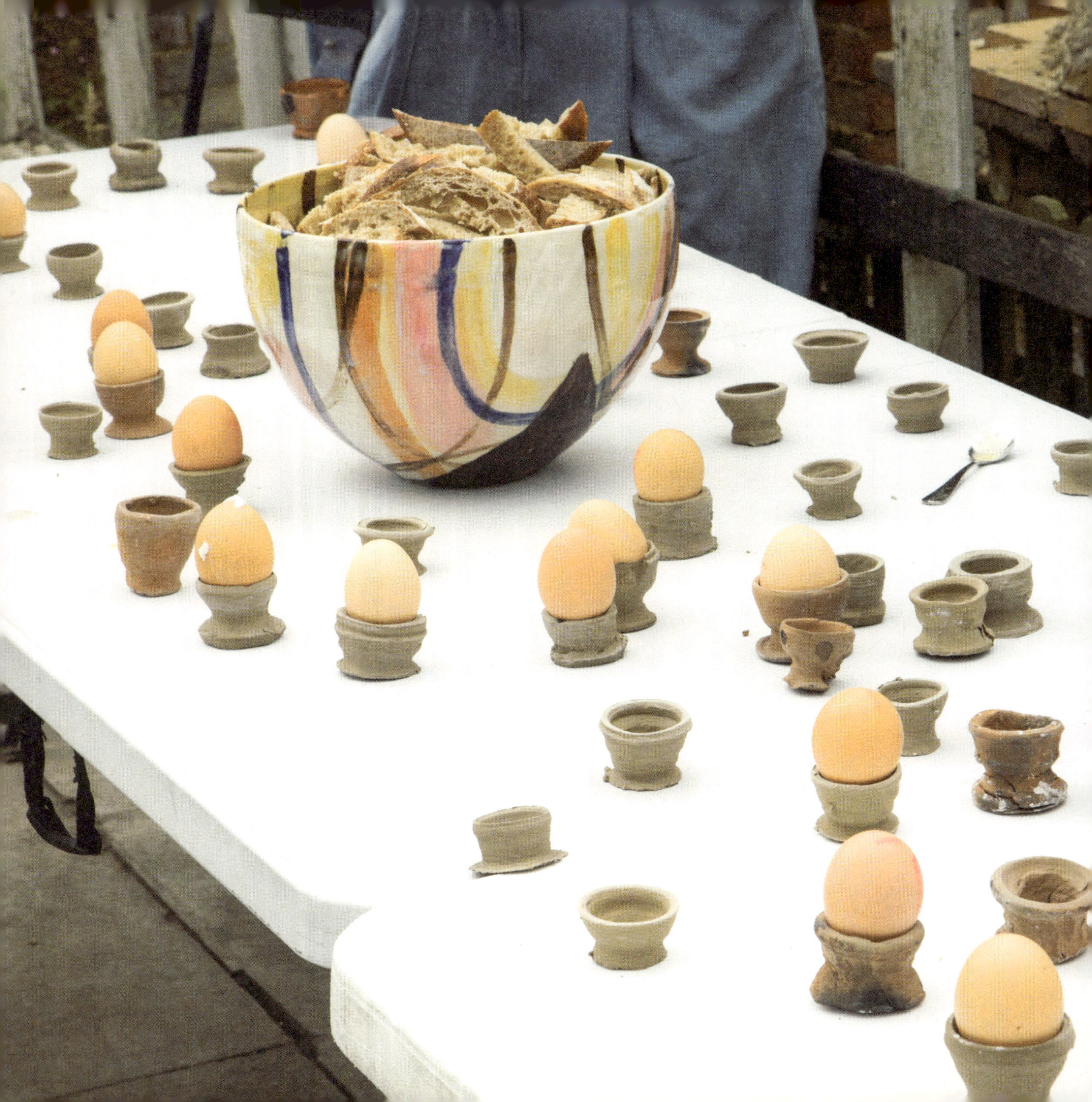

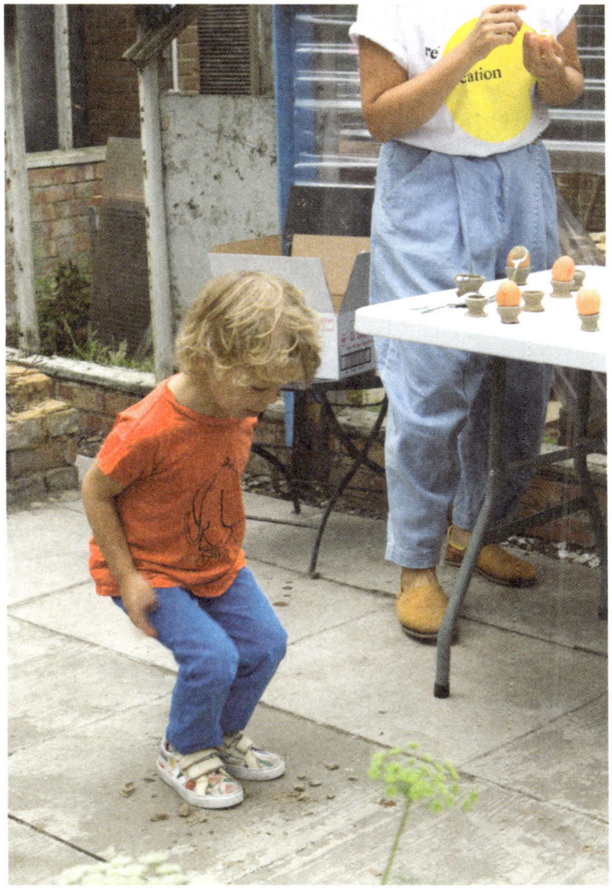

Introduction
Francesca Anfossi

During the nineteenth century, a plant nursery was established in the garden at the centre of Rochester Square. From the early 1920s to the late 1980s, this nursery was home to Strouds, a film-props company that specialised in supplying palm trees to the entertainment industry. When the company went out of business, the site was abandoned and then squatted by various groups for over twenty-five years. In 2016, my husband Eric and I had the opportunity to acquire the derelict land and its buildings and turn it into an arts-and-crafts centre for the local community.

Since we took over the site, I have been managing its day-to-day operations together with artists and friends. I have established a large ceramics studio open to professional and amateur potters and hosted artist residencies and collaborations with local primary schools and national universities. Every other month, Rochester Square hosts a communal dinner open to all, an occasion for neighbours from all walks of life to meet and share ideas about the square's future. The former plant nursery is still largely derelict, and Eric and I are exploring various ways to restore it, working with Camden Council and the award-winning architecture studio 6a.

Those active in the square are a mixed group, thirty artists and makers from London ranging from twenty to eighty years old who need a space to make, think and be together in a relaxing and creative atmosphere. Togetherness is what you breathe in Rochester Square. I try to connect with others by sharing food with our Monday 'family' lunches, working collaboratively when there is the opportunity and engaging in other social projects.

After I started working with clay ten years ago, I struggled to find the right facilities where I could learn and experiment with the material – it is not an easy process to do on your own. More generally, in my artistic practice I engage with people in projects that often involve cooking and eating together as ways to share an everyday, yet fundamental, activity. When my husband and I saw the abandoned site of Rochester Square, I realised this could be an amazing chance to bring together something that was missing, in terms of combining ceramics facilities with my interest in socially engaged projects.

Rochester Square is an actual square located between a large council estate and rows of expensive residential homes. When walking by during my many years as a local resident, I always had the impression that the site was separating the two worlds rather than bringing them together as a classic square would. Acquiring the site, our idea was to turn it into an engine for local social life. People tell me that they had never met their neighbour before they came to one of our communal dinners, and I just love that we can make this happen. There is great meaning for us in creating a space that can become a catalyst for people to meet through the powerful yet simple tool of making things together or sharing a meal.

For now, the main activity of the site is focused on clay, the garden and food. I believe that in a city like London, where the social needs of communities are often overridden by financial interests, a space like this sets out a different model for cohabitation and social interaction based on reconnecting with raw materials and the creative exchange of practical knowledge. Throughout the last five years, many local residents have been visiting, eating, cooking and attending ceramic classes here. There is a constant coming and going of people and a supportive group of local artists suggesting projects and developing ideas both big and small inside the warehouse and outside in the garden areas. Local schools have also been involved in our programme, and we have run workshops with children from primary schools. I feel that the square functions based on a strong reciprocity: we offer opportunities to local residents and institutions, and they give back by contributing new ideas.

Through working with clay, I have realised how adaptable, inclusive and nonhierarchical it is. We use it every day for one of our most basic activities – in the form of tableware for eating. From children's education to making art, from architectural experimentation to crafts therapy, clay can be both a humble and a highly sophisticated material. Furthermore, ceramics, like many crafts, is inherently communal: technical progress on an individual level is often obtained through the exchange of practical knowledge with others.

My main vision for Rochester Square came from a trip I made to India some years ago. I was fascinated by the system there of recycling clay teacups: fired at very low temperatures, they are very friable and are smashed to the ground after use, easily turning back into soil which is then used again to make new teacups. This image stuck with me, and it guides my approach to Rochester Square: a sort of creative earth cycle from soil (clay) to plants (food) to plates (eating). My long-term dream is to create a contemporary, more interactive version of a sculpture garden, a place where art installations, plants and crafts can offer recreational and artistic activities to people of all ages.

This book is the eclectic record of the amazing production of the people of Rochester Square – their ceramics, recipes, garden photos and drawings – a rich testament that forms its legacy.

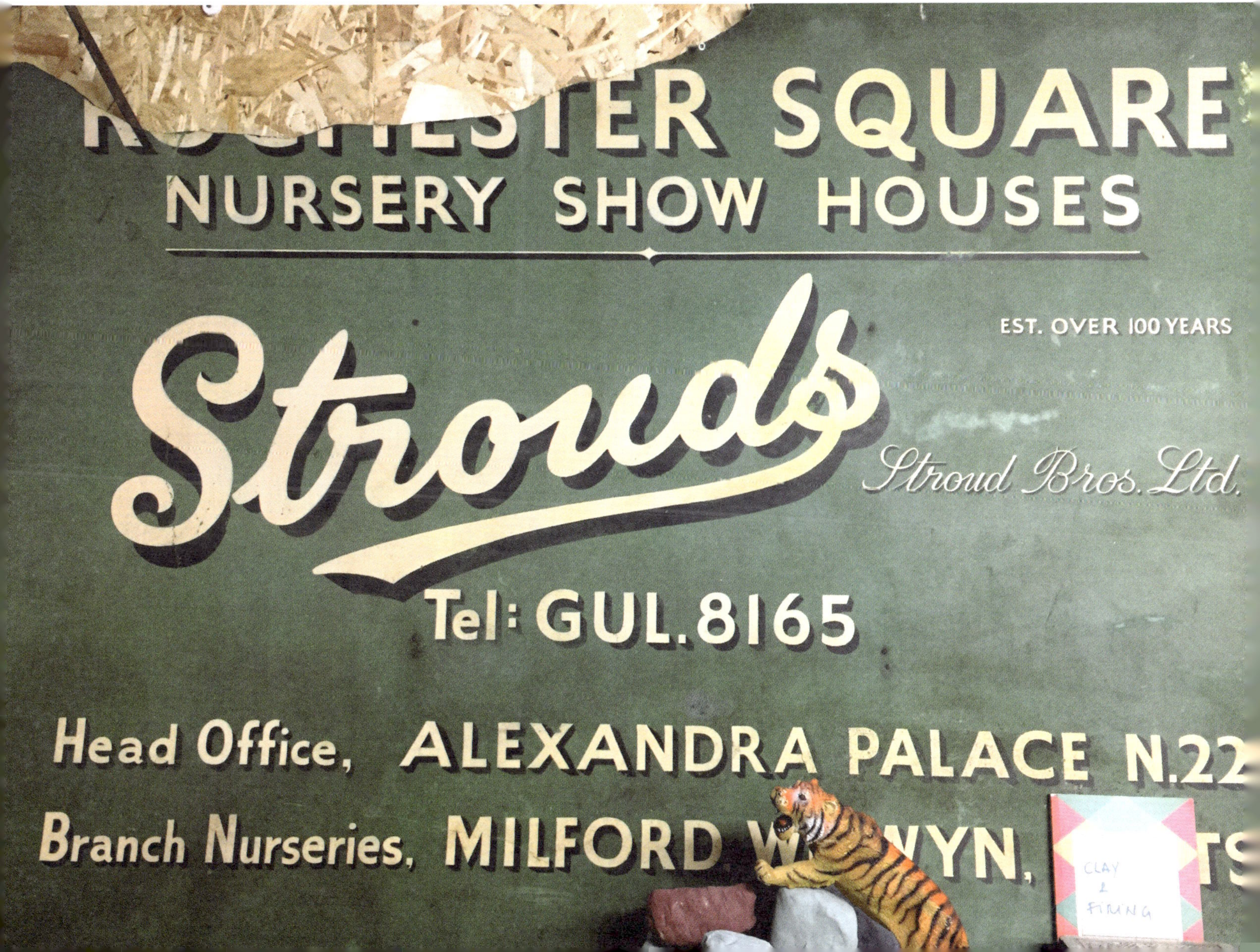
SQUARE
NURSERY SHOW HOUSES
Strouds
EST. OVER 100 YEARS
Stroud Bros. Ltd.
Tel: GUL. 8165
Head Office, ALEXANDRA PALACE N.22
Branch Nurseries, MILFORD
WYN,
CLAY
&
FIRING

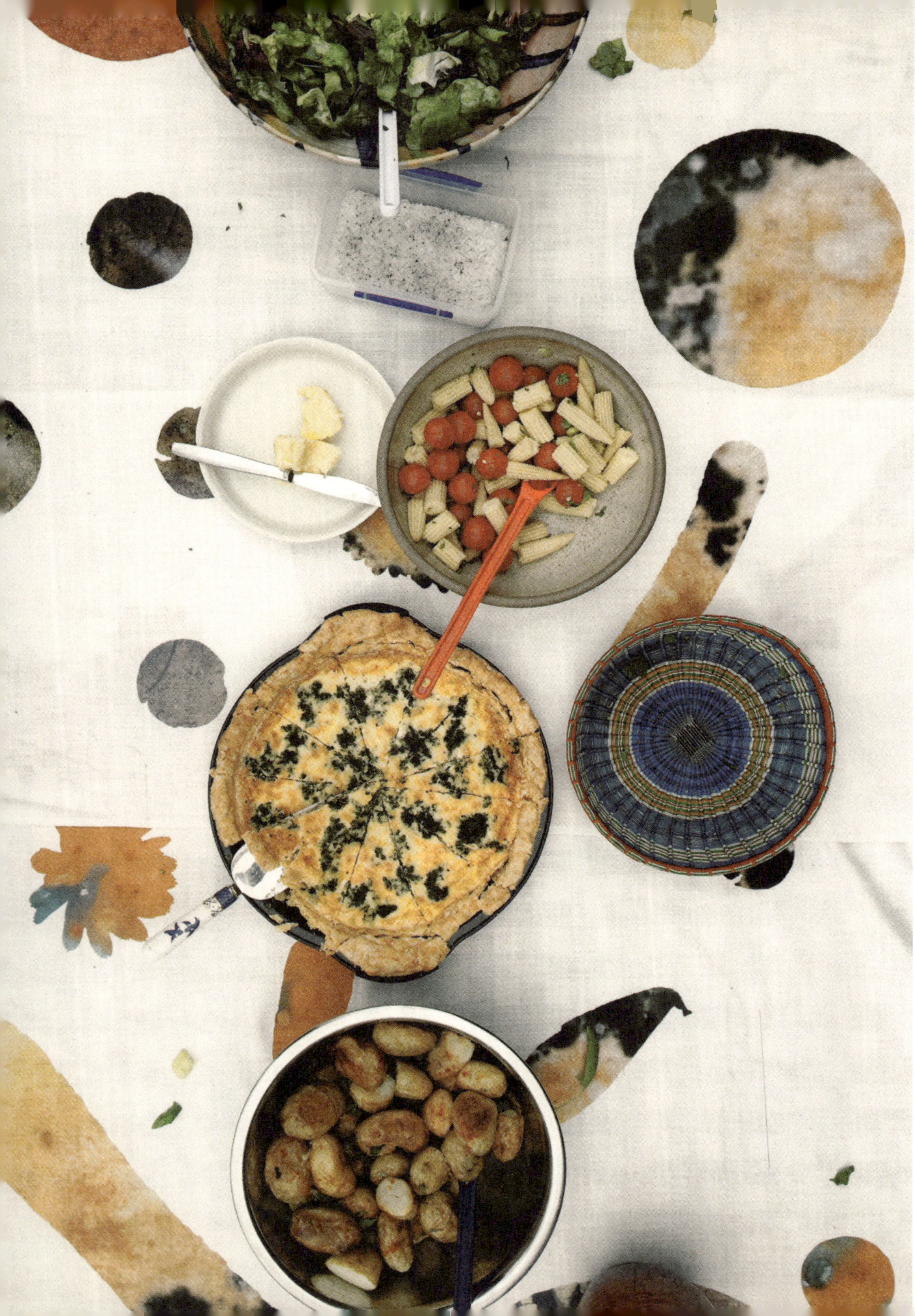

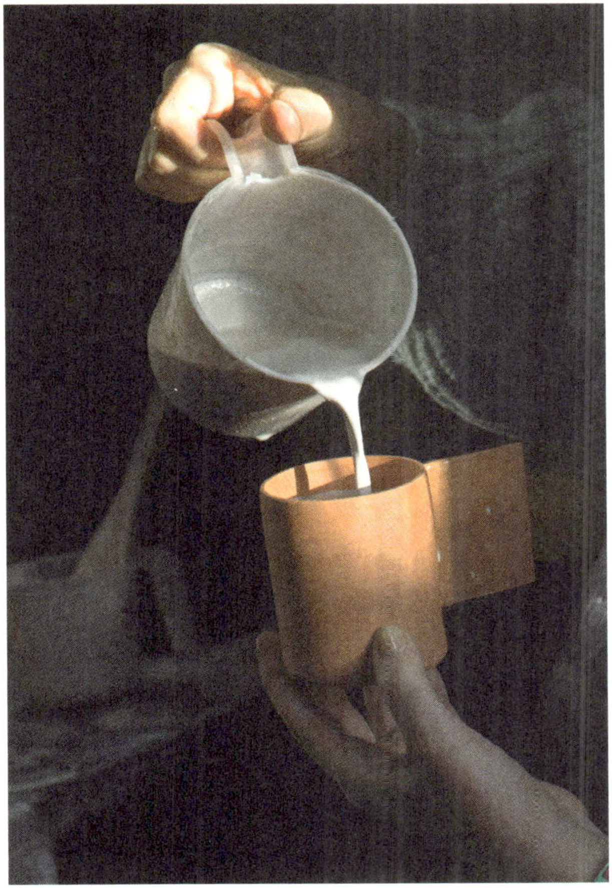

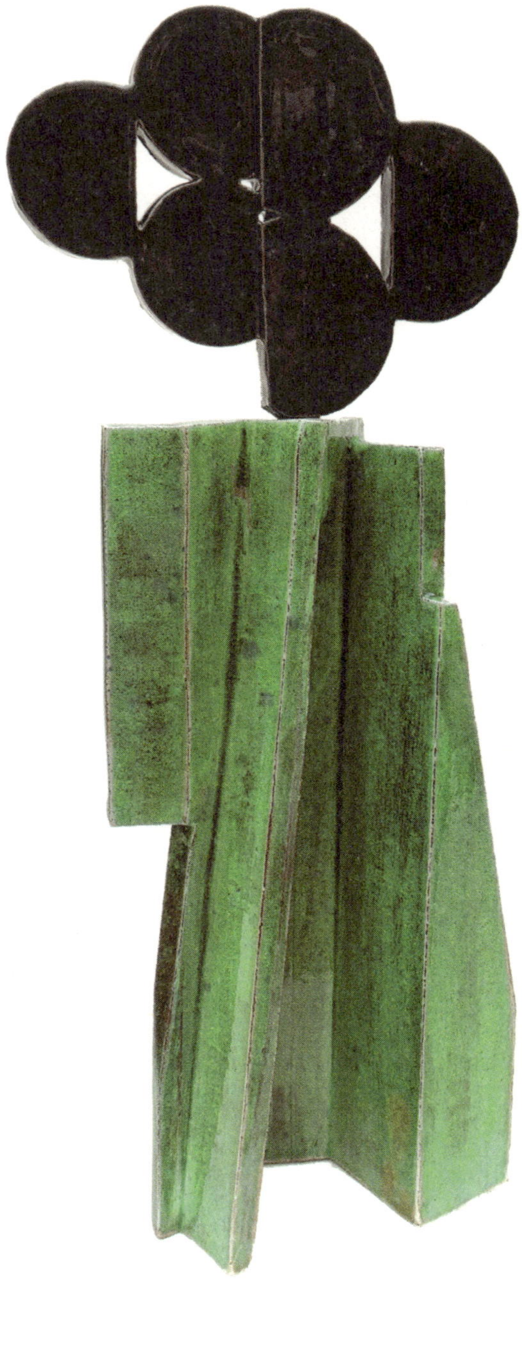

Aude Van Ryn, 2020

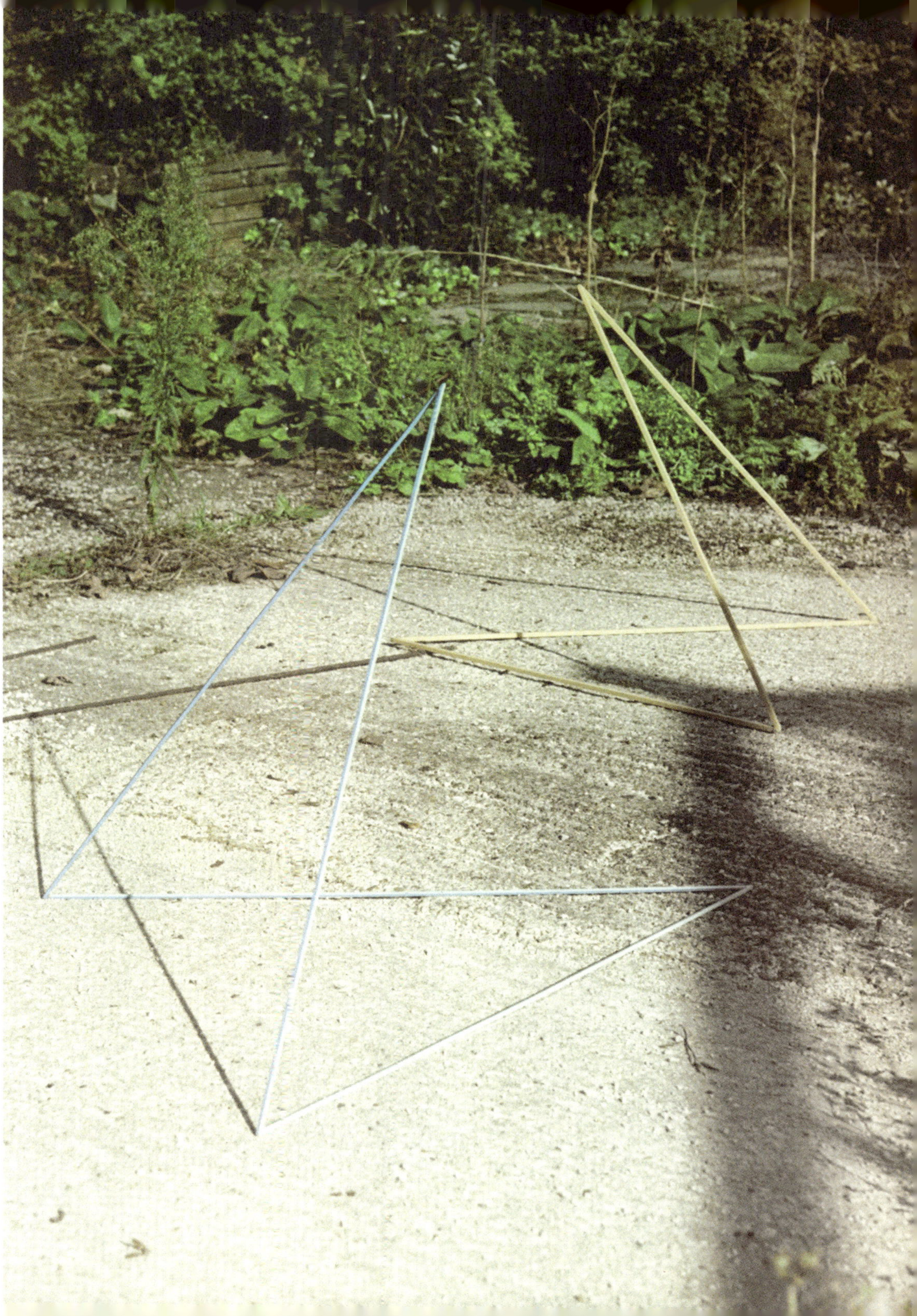

Lilah Fowler, 2019

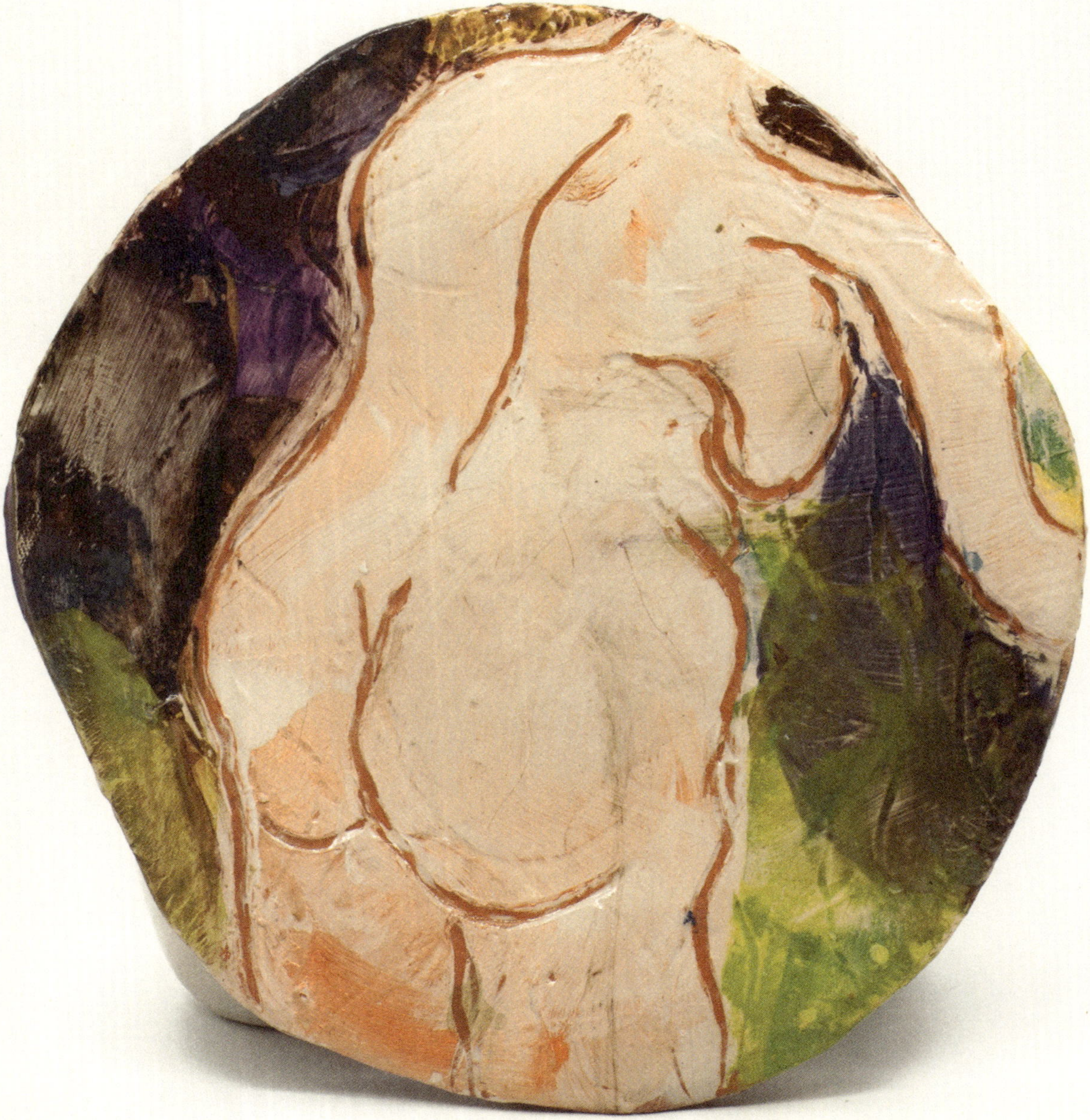

Anne Ryan, 2021

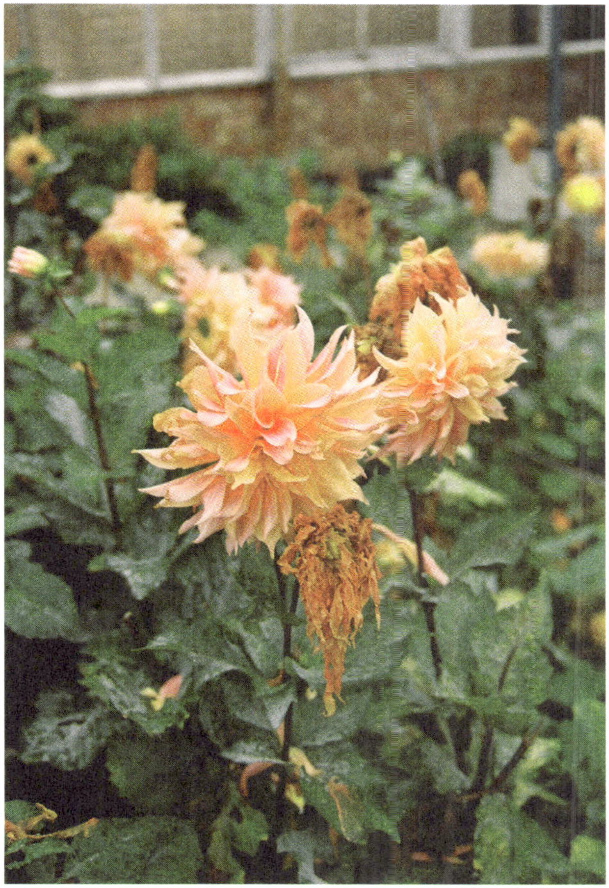

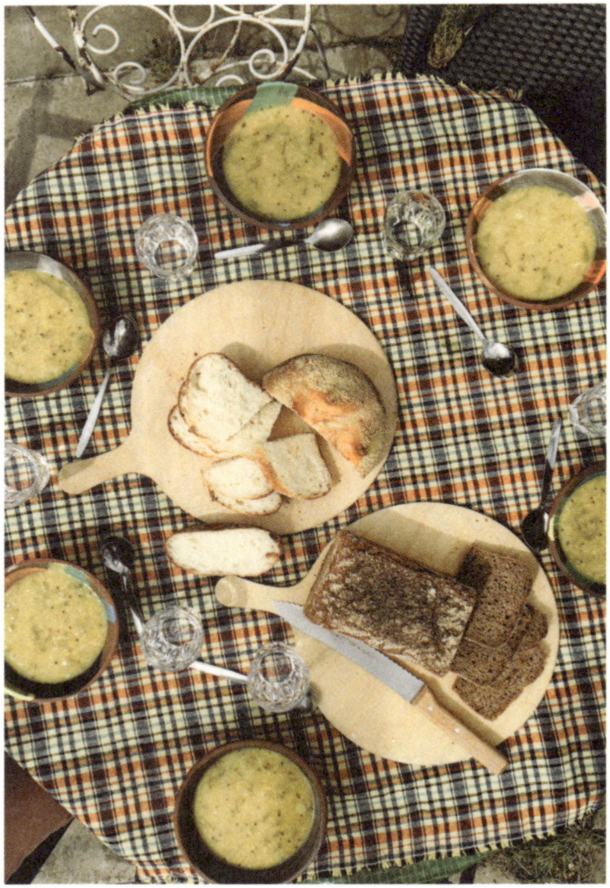

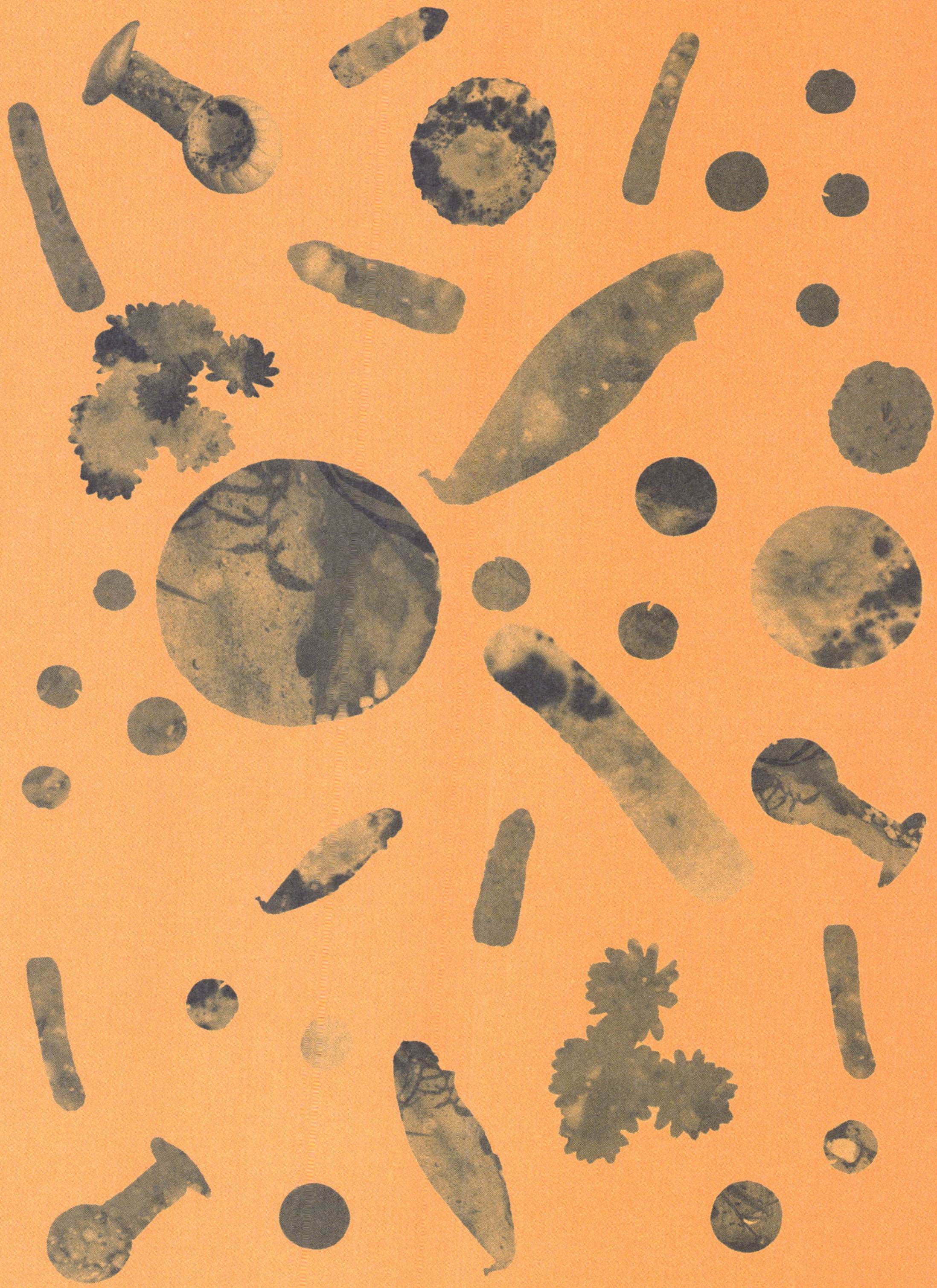

Francesca Anfossi, 2019

New Recipes for Society
Chris Fite-Wassilak

The table is mountained with glasses, jugs and plates, fragments of food and irregular vases filled with fruit. In your bowl are the remnants of a stew, the dark stain of sauce indistinguishable from the dashes of paint that decorate the dish. You might reach to pick up a piece of flatbread sat on the tablecloth to mop things up, seeing its rounded, uneven edges, to find it surprisingly heavy: another camouflaged serving plate. Shards of cheese mimic the triangular appendages of the vessels that sit next to them. Anything semi-solid that might hold some liquid is taken up as a cup. The meals and gatherings at Rochester Square are an overflowing confusion of textures and tastes, crossed conversations and elbows bumped over long tables and communal platters, all nestled amongst the pottery wheels and busy shelves of the ceramic studio.

Clay, as an artistic medium, is often remarked upon for its visceral, tactile qualities: a messy, primal dough that starts with a luscious wetness and bakes to a brittle crust. It has a natural proximity to cooking, to the squishing and kneading and transformations of food. The activities and rhythms of the square add their own idiosyncratic spin to this ancient alliance of clay and food: it celebrates their association and plays off their similarities, their shared smells, textures and appearances, to see what else might come from throwing them together. The artists working and eating here have a wide range of approaches but the project of Rochester Square turns this constant mingling into a wider, ongoing event-based artwork.

Food, as an artistic medium, is a bit more slippery. Food makes complex negotiations of taste and identity, mediating a network of sources and interpersonal relationships; which is to say, food already achieves many of the aims of contemporary art. Anthropologist of etiquette Margaret Visser, in her book *The Rituals of Dinner* (1991), refers to food as a 'mythic prototype': something that both nourishes and carries all sorts of other meanings and gestures, a para-medium of sorts. Within Rochester Square, it becomes a medium with which to attract people at certain points in time, a way to ask what makes a group, an assembly or a community for however brief a moment. It's an issue that might start practically – we all need to eat – but in the manners and means of fulfilling that need, it brings other things to the table, so to speak.

'We use eating as a medium for social relationships: satisfaction of the most individual of needs becomes a means of creating community', Visser states. Though what constitutes community in eating is a complex back-and-forth of intentions and incident: food, in any city, relies on a dense web of supply and distribution, a sort of dispersed, spectral community that hovers around any bite taken. Rochester Square is in the heart of Camden, a dense and muddled part of London – despite its garden idyll, it is very much an urban context inhabited by urban creatures. Our 'individual needs' are never just individually met: we don't grow our own vegetables or rear our own animals, or make our own pots to cook in, our own silverware or plates. The things unfolding at the square short-circuit some of those supply chains and become a more active means of re-asserting community as a choice, with food being served and eaten from objects made on-site, some of which were made from the London clay on-site – and often you'll find yourself sitting next to the person who made your crumb-sprinkled plate. These various linkages start to indicate a sense of connection, and a sense of possibility, in how we eat.

For Visser, the sharing of food is the basis for society itself and the heart of the human sense of morality. Table manners codify complex social interchanges, and the harmony of sharing a meal always comes at a cost: who isn't there, what can't be said, what can't be eaten. Rochester Square's eating rules and patterns are deceptively simple: members of the ceramic studio eat together every week, taking turns cooking for each other. Every other month, the square hosts a wider communal dinner, where one or two people prepare a meal for a larger group of loosely invited guests: neighbours, friends, collaborators, potential collaborators or people simply interested in what goes on there. The communal dinner is a one-pot meal – a soup, a stew, anything that can be made easily for several dozen people. Guests are asked to bring their own drinks, contribute a fiver to the costs of the meal and, once the food is dished out, the rest is up to them: seating is a free-for-all, discussion is free-flowing and how the evening proceeds is open-ended. Attending these dinners has its responsibilities – not just in making conversation with new people, but also the rule that anyone who has come to three communal dinners has to cook one of the following. Even if this rule has, so far, never been strictly followed, it's a useful reminder to everyone there that being a guest is an active role, that you are participating in creating something that is shaped by your being there.

The meals themselves that have been cooked over the course of the communal dinners are also reflective of the type of community being formed: from Greek bean soup to red lentil dal, Thai curry to Catalan beef stew, the singular pot holds an international spread that shows how multiple ingredients can be combined and multiple mouths fed. These dinners also speak about how food seeps across borders: bean chilli is a loosely Tex-Mex dish, an adaptable mix of ingredients that originated with itinerant workers somewhere around the US-Mexican border, and has since been changed around the world with whatever is to hand. Japanese curry is a mild, thick curry that was a British adaptation of bolder Indian curries based on the British colonial presence on the subcontinent and introduced by the British to Japan at some point in the nineteenth century. In the melting pot of London, these intricate politics find further expression and new combinations.

Dan Jurafsky, in his book *The Language of Food* (2014), proposes a 'grammar of cuisine' – meal structures are like a language, and established rules and consensus create a notion of what is appropriate, permissible and understandable as part of a dish or meal. Thus, how in China there's no conception of 'dessert' as such, but meals are viewed as a combination of a starch staple with a range of non-starch dishes; or how Italians have such inordinately strict feelings about combining cheese with fish; or how Americans eat salad at the start of the meal, while Europeans resolutely eat salad after their main course. He sets out a series of mock equations for national meal grammars: Italy = antipasto, primo, secondo, salad, dessert; China = starch + non-starch. Through the square's rhythm of gatherings, with the meals and regular punctuation of event days, all of which are mediated and guided by open tables of food and earthenware, it's apparent that co-mingling is programmed into Rochester Square's ongoing identity: meeting new people over food, sharing space and food in order to share a moment. Following this, we might propose that the square's equation is obviously simple: clay + pot of food. But in that simplicity is an instruction, an imperative to be together, where Rochester Square is host to an attempt to create a new grammar and develop its own communal language.

Minestrone alla genovese for Lots of People!
Francesca Anfossi

SERVES 12

5 aubergines
8 tomatoes
4 large handfuls of French beans
1 head of cabbage
10 courgettes
1 broccoli
3 large bunches of chard or spinach
10 onions
2 bunches of celery
10 carrots
2 bunches of marjoram
4 bay leaves
4–5 400-gram cans of borlotti beans
5–6 potatoes, cubed
pasta (ditalini rigati or other small-shaped pasta)

I measure the amount of ingredients in this recipe by eye and taste. Adapt to your liking.

Cut aubergines, tomatoes, French beans, cabbage, courgettes, broccoli and chard or spinach into small pieces and add to a large pot filled halfway with boiling water. Boil for one hour.

Finely dice the onion, celery, and carrots. Sauté in oil and add to pot, together with the marjoram and bay leaves.

After the vegetables have boiled for one hour, take the bay leaves out and blend with a hand blender in bursts; gradually add more boiling water to achieve a liquid consistency. Add the borlotti beans, potatoes and pasta (around 25 grams per person). Bring to a boil, until the pasta is cooked, around 15–20 minutes.

Before serving, add a bit of handmade pesto, Parmesan cheese and good olive oil … *e buon appetito!* Be careful not to burn the roof of your mouth!

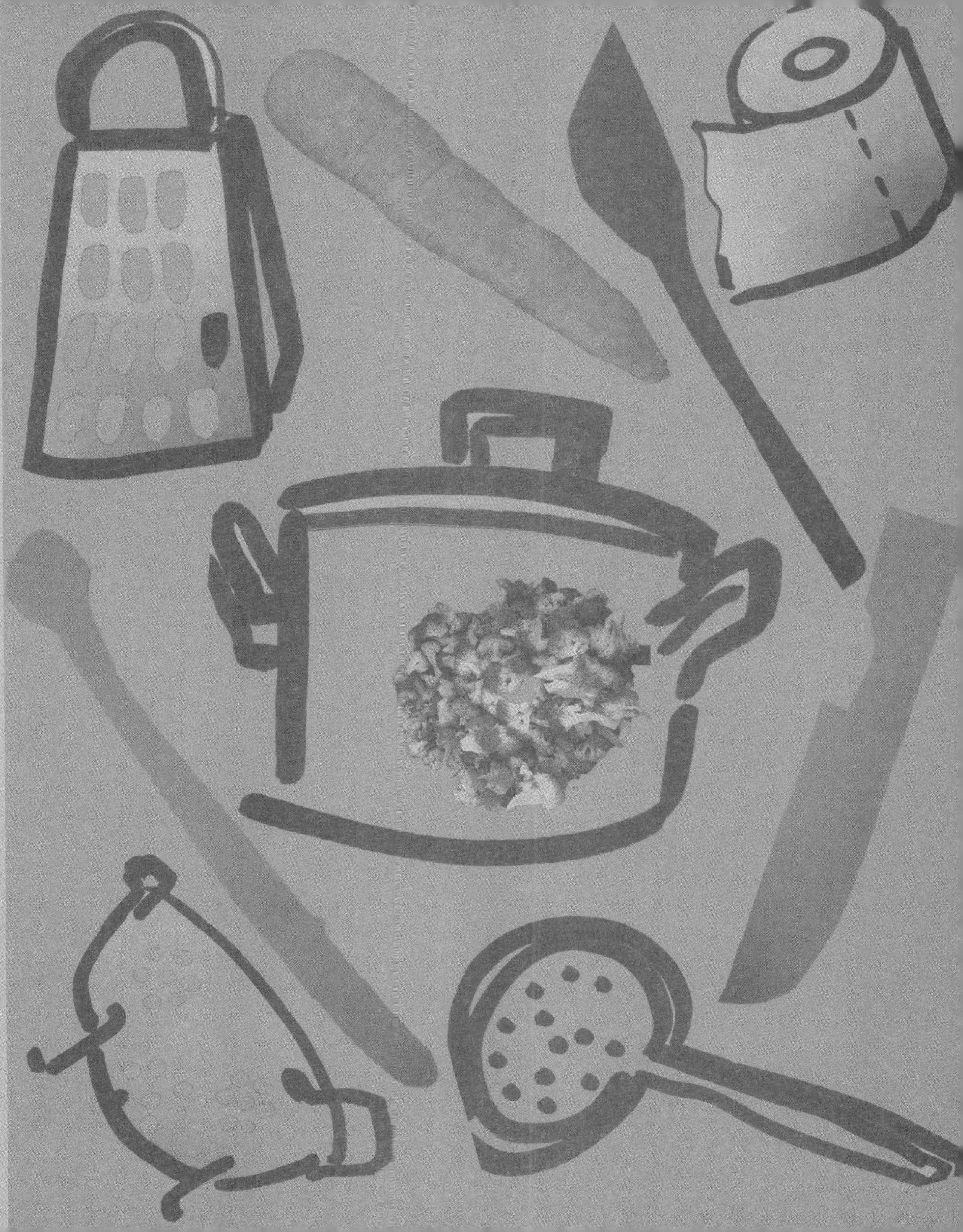

Vegetarian Bean Chilli
Fanny Singer and Filipa Ramos

SERVES 12

2 cups cooked black-eyed peas
2 cups cooked black beans
2 cups cooked pinto or borlotti beans
2 cups cooked chickpeas
2 cups red kidney beans
4 stalks celery, chopped
4 carrots peeled, cut into ¼ inch rounds
2 medium onions, diced
4 bell peppers deseeded and diced into ½-inch pieces (red, yellow, orange make a nice mix of colours)
1 head of garlic, peeled and minced
2 sweet potatoes, peeled and cubed (½ inch)
1 small butternut squash, skin peeled, seeds scooped, cubed (½ inch)
2 cans peeled tomatoes
4 cups broth (vegetable or chicken)
1 handful of chopped coriander leaves
2 tablespoons powdered unsweetened cocoa powder
1 tablespoon chilli powder
½ teaspoon ground cinnamon
½ teaspoon sweet smoked paprika
1 teaspoon ground cumin
1 teaspoon cumin seeds
¼ teaspoon ground coriander
¼ teaspoon coriander seeds
¼ teaspoon fennel seeds
¼ teaspoon ground black pepper
1 tablespoon fine sea salt

Our chilli is a very loose version of a classic vegetarian bean chilli. Serve with buckwheat cornbread.

Cook beans in advance in separate pots or use well-drained, high-quality canned versions of a mix of beans. You can use the kinds of dry beans you like best, but the varieties in the ingredients list are easy enough to source at most grocers. Interesting varieties of heirloom beans make wonderful chillis, if you can find them.

Sauté the celery, carrots, onions, bell peppers and garlic in a big glug of extra virgin olive oil until soft, translucent and fragrant.

Meanwhile, coat sweet potatoes and butternut squash in olive oil and salt and black pepper, and roast at 180°C until tender and lightly browned.

Add the sweet potatoes and squash to the celery/carrot/onion mixture, then add tomatoes, broth and coriander leaves.

Stir, then add the spices (cocoa powder, chilli powder, ground cinnamon, smoked paprika, ground cumin, cumin seeds, ground coriander, coriander seeds, fennel seeds, ground black pepper, sea salt).

Allow to simmer together for an hour or two until the spices and flavours are well married and the beans and vegetables are cooked but not mushy. Add more broth or water if it feels too dry or too thick. Adjust the spices and salt if necessary.

Mix a cup of thick plain unsweetened yogurt with the zest and juice of one lemon, a handful of finely minced chives, a big pinch of salt and plenty of black pepper. Roughly chop a bunch of fresh coriander.

Serve the chilli with a dollop of yogurt and a sprinkle of coriander leaves.

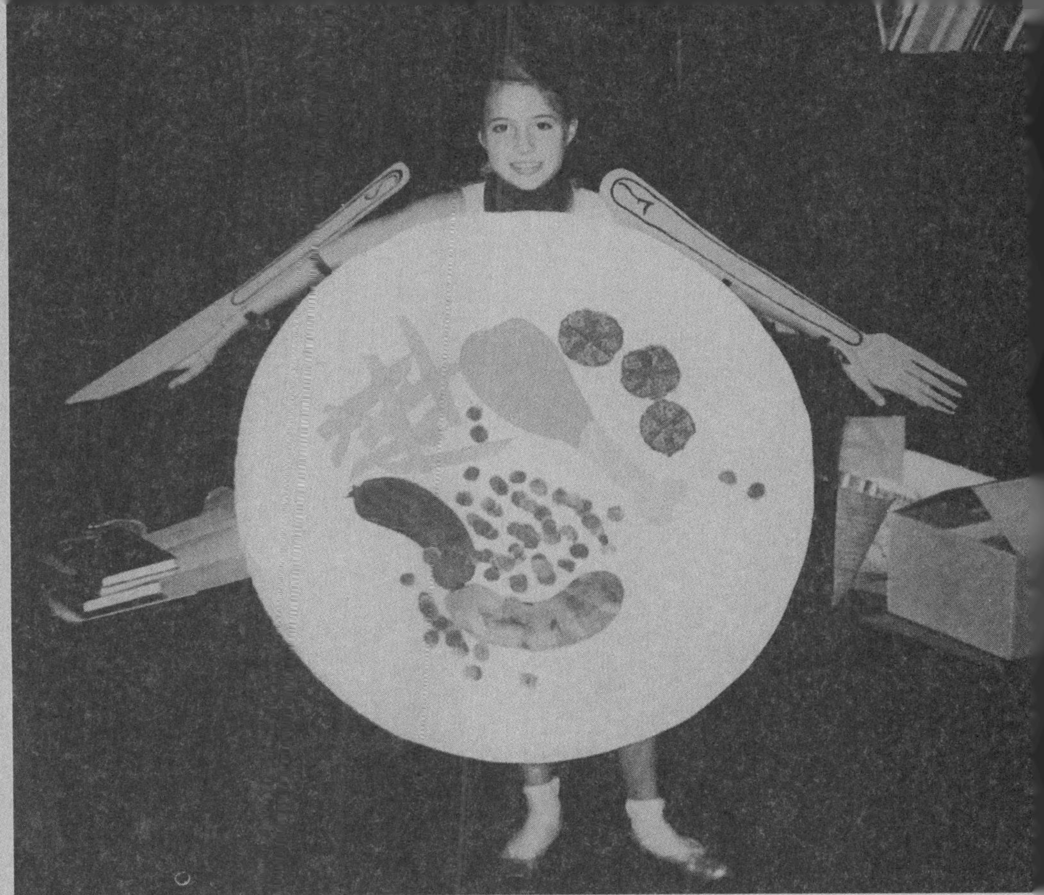

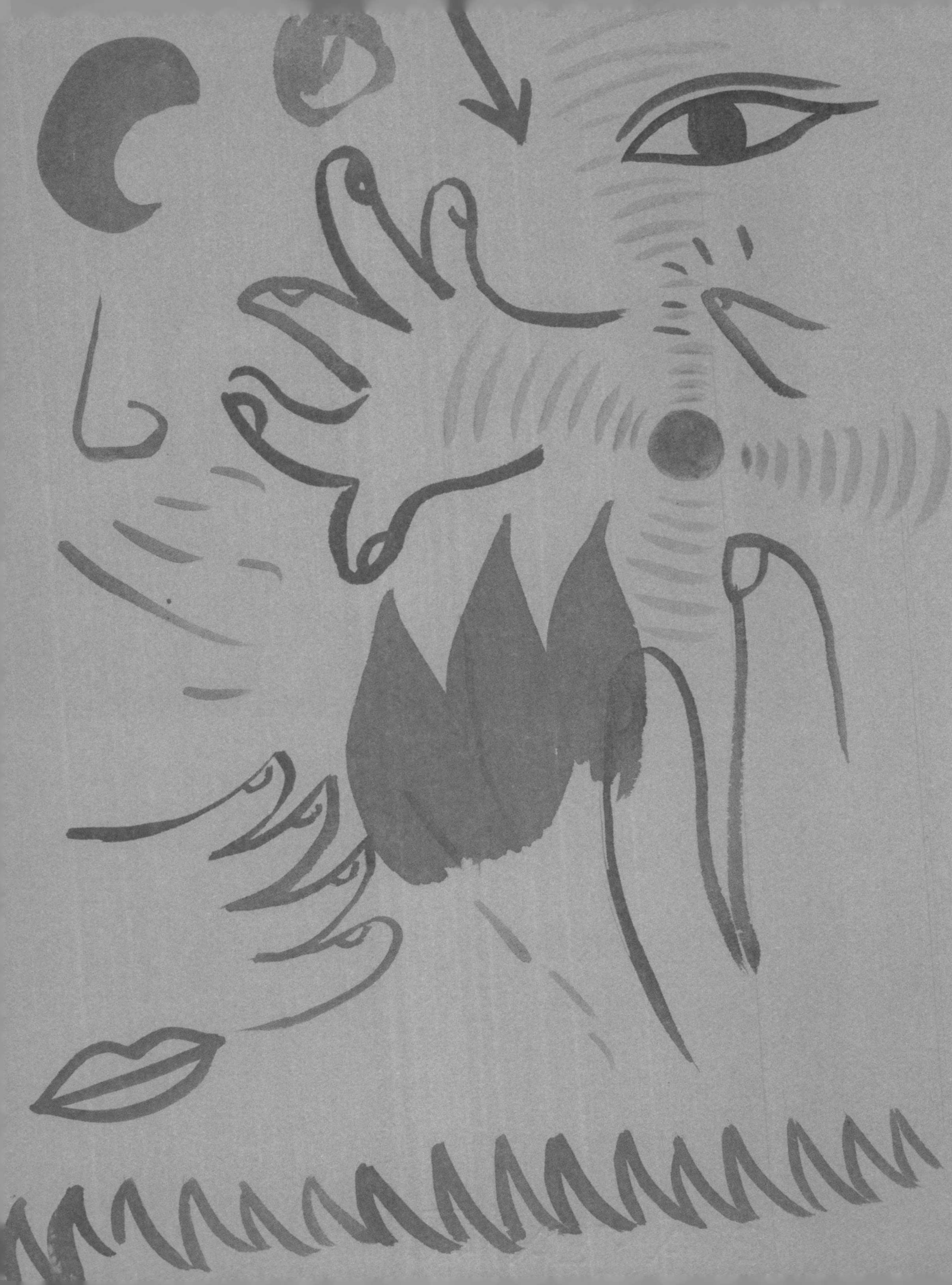

Coconut Chickpea Curry
Paulina Michnowska

SERVES 30

10 tablespoons coconut oil
10 medium yellow onions, sliced
2 kilograms fresh tomatoes, diced
(if using canned, drain the tomatoes)
sea salt & ground black pepper, to taste
2 kilograms canned chickpeas, drained
15 garlic cloves, minced
7½ tablespoons garam masala
5 teaspoons curry powder
5 teaspoons cumin
2 kilograms canned coconut milk
10 teaspoons coconut flour
10–15 small limes

In a deep pot over medium high heat, add the coconut oil.

Add the onions and tomatoes. Grind some sea salt and black pepper over the mixture and stir. Lower heat to medium and allow to cook down until the juices of the tomatoes have been released and the onions are soft, about 10 minutes.

Add the chickpeas, garlic, garam masala, curry powder and cumin.
Stir to combine.

Add the coconut milk and stir again. Add the coconut flour, which helps to slightly thicken the curry. Bring to a boil and then reduce heat to medium-low and simmer for 10–12 minutes.

Taste the curry and season with salt and pepper if you desire. Remove from heat and squeeze the limes lightly over the curry, stirring to combine.

One Pot Wonder
Spicy Coconut and Lentil Dal
Hattie Spires

SERVES 4

FOR THE ONE POT WONDER

1 glug olive oil
2 red onions, finely chopped
360 grams boneless, free-range chicken thighs, cut into bite-size pieces
2 400-gram cans chopped tomatoes
good dash of Worcestershire sauce
100 millilitres crème fraîche
big bag of spinach
1 400-gram can butter beans
1 bunch fresh basil

FOR THE DAL

400 grams dry green lentils
2 400-millilitre cans coconut milk
3 garlic cloves, minced
2 large tomatoes, chopped
1 teaspoon cumin
1 teaspoon curry powder
1 teaspoon cinnamon
1 teaspoon paprika
1 teaspoon chilli powder
1 handful chilli flakes
to serve: rice, coconut yogurt, chilli flakes

ONE POT WONDER

Heat the olive oil in a large casserole over medium heat. Sweat the onions, then add the chicken and sauté for 5 minutes. Add the tomatoes and Worcestershire sauce and simmer for 15 minutes.

Stir in the crème fraîche, spinach and butter beans and simmer for 5 minutes, until the chicken is cooked through.

Season to taste and stir in the basil to serve.

SPICY COCONUT AND LENTIL DAL

Put all ingredients into a big pan and give it a good stir. Bring to a boil before reducing the heat to a simmer. Season with salt and pepper, to taste. Leave uncovered for 2–3 hours, until thick, making sure to add more water if the dal starts to stick to the bottom of the pan.

Add more cans of coconut milk and top up with water if cooking for, say … 30 or so people!

When the dal is almost cooked, put the rice on.

Once the dal is ready, stir in extra salt.

Serve with rice, a dollop of coconut yogurt and a sprinkling of chilli flakes.

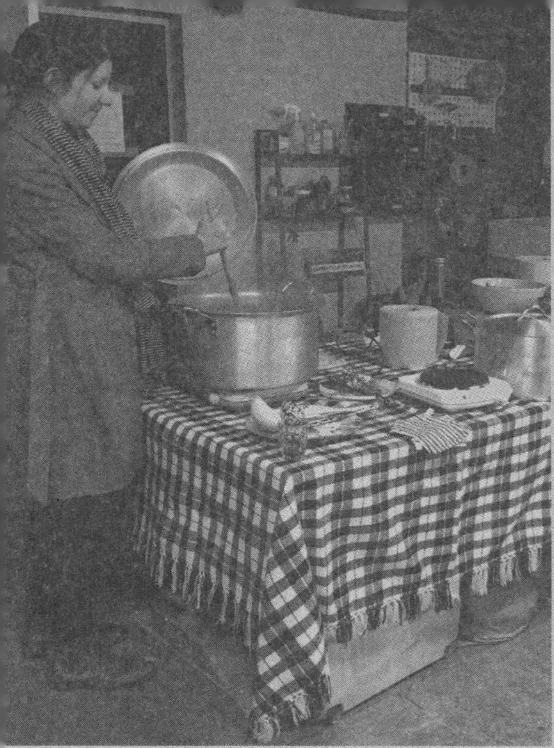

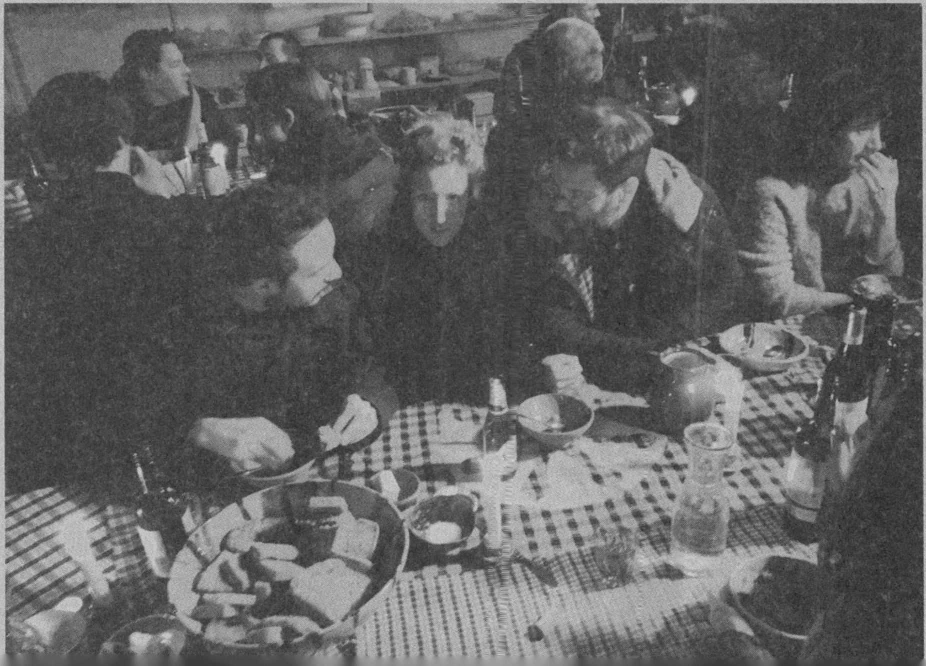

Courgette and White Bean Stew
Anna Tobias

SERVES 4

200 grams dried white beans, preferably cannellini or cocco bianco
1 head garlic
1 sprig sage
800 grams courgette
3 plum tomatoes, peeled and chopped, or half a can of chopped tomatoes
1 bunch basil, leaves picked
1 lemon
5 tablespoons cooking olive oil
8 tablespoons good quality olive oil
salt and pepper

Cover the beans in cold water by 2 inches and leave to soak overnight.

The next day, drain the beans, place them in a roomy saucepan and cover them with fresh cold water by 1 inch. Place half the bulb of garlic in the pot along with the sprig of sage.

Bring to a boil and skim off any scum that appears. Lower the heat and allow to gently bubble away for about 1–1.5 hours, until the beans are cooked. The beans should be soft and yielding and not have any bite. If they still feel a little resistant then simmer a little longer.

Discard the sage. Fish out the garlic and squeeze the cloves from their skins. Mash them up with a fork and stir the pulp back into the beans. Season generously with salt and pepper and stir in 4 tablespoons of the good olive oil.

Slice the courgette into rounds the thickness of a pound coin. Finely chop 4 cloves of garlic.

In a wide saucepan, heat the cooking olive oil until very hot. Add the courgette and stir to coat the slices in oil. Leave on medium-high heat and cover with a lid. Stir every 2 minutes for 8 minutes.

By this time, the courgette should have slacked a bit but maintained a good colour. Add the garlic and stir for 1 or 2 minutes until it has softened.

Now add the tomatoes and let cook gently for 20 minutes. At this point, add the basil and cook for 2 minutes.

Drain the beans in a colander over a bowl to keep the liquid.

Stir the beans in with the courgette and add enough of the bean liquid (about a third) so you have a sloppy and luscious stew.

Right before serving, and off the heat, stir in the remaining good olive oil and zest the lemon over the stew.

This dish is best served warm, not hot.

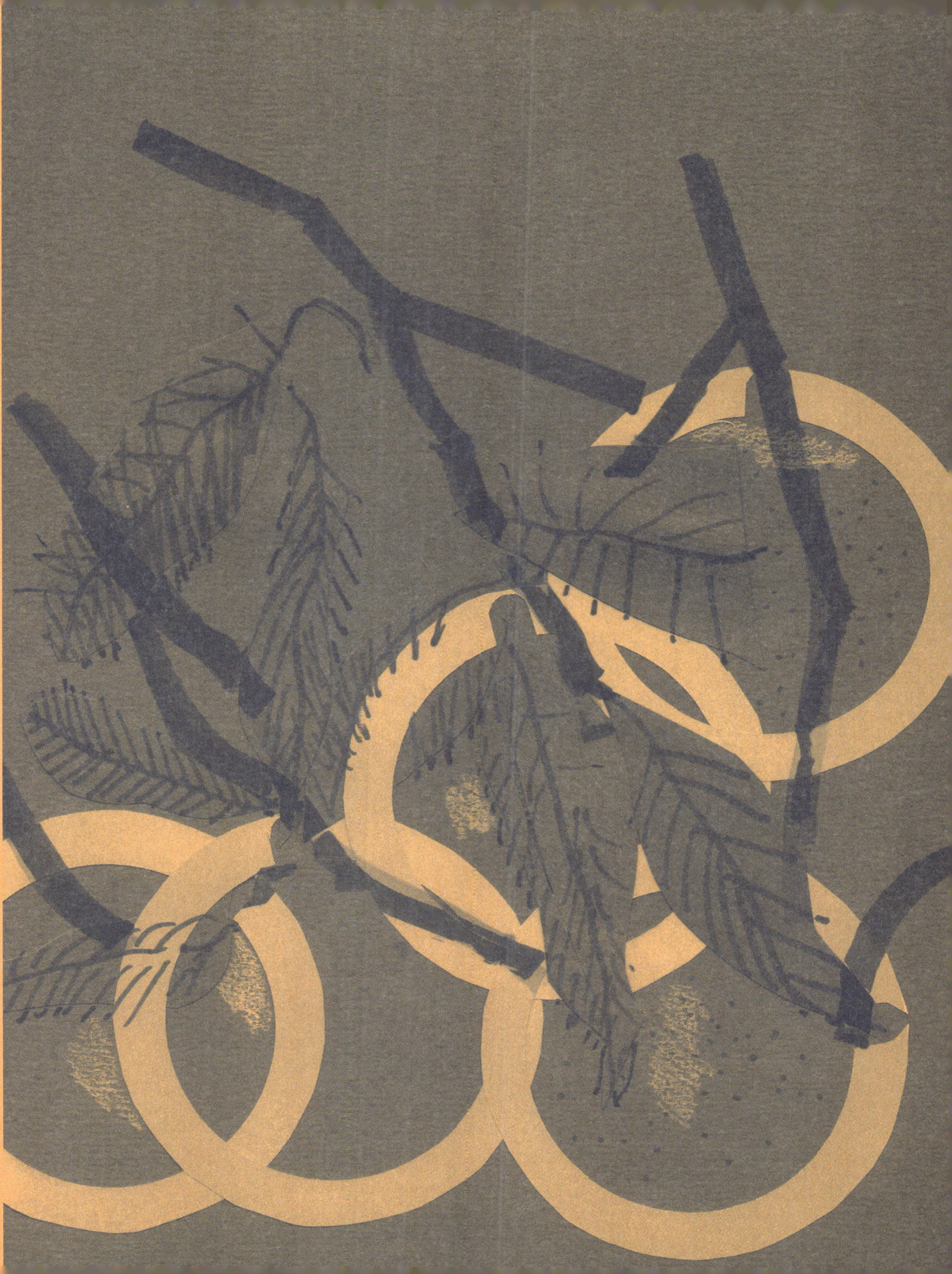

La Grotta Ice's Blood Orange Sorbet Kitty Travers

SERVES 4

155 grams unrefined sugar
255 grams water
4 blood oranges (fridge-cold)
1 unwaxed lemon (fridge-cold)

In a small pan, heat the sugar and water, stirring until the sugar dissolves, then remove from heat.

Add the grated zest of one orange and the grated zest of the lemon to the syrup and leave to cool, then chill in the fridge for at least 2 hours or overnight.

Juice the oranges and lemon and add the juice to the cold syrup. Blitz thoroughly in a blender before straining through a sieve. Squeeze the zest to extract all the volatile oils.

Pour mix into an ice cream machine and churn for 20–25 minutes until thick, snowy and pale pink.

Transfer the sorbet to a lidded container. Top with a piece of waxed paper and freeze until ready to serve. Best eaten same day; keeps well for a fortnight in the freezer.

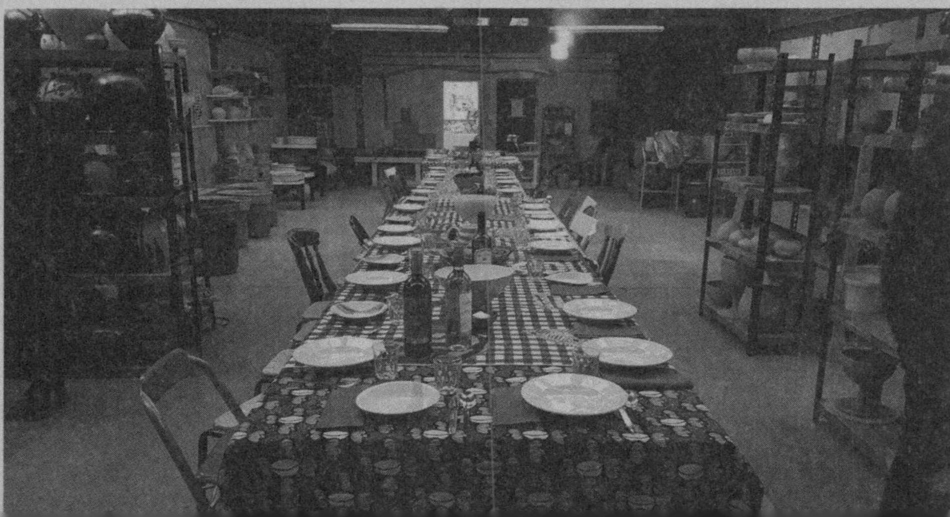

Japanese Curry
Nissa Nishikawa

SERVES 30

extra virgin olive oil
garlic
ginger
fried tofu*
purple onions*
aubergines*
mushrooms*
courgettes*
carrots*
purple sweet potatoes*
kale*
broccoli*
water
5 packages of Golden Curry (mild)
short-grain brown rice
coriander & spring onions for garnish

Improvise amounts based on preference.
*organic

In a large pot, gently sauté garlic, ginger and onions in oil.

Fill pot halfway with water. Bring to a boil.

Add tofu and all vegetables except kale and broccoli.

Boil for 15 minutes and then add kale and broccoli.

Add Golden Curry.

Boil until Golden Curry is dissolved and the water has thickened.

Serve with short-grain brown rice and garnish with coriander and spring onions.

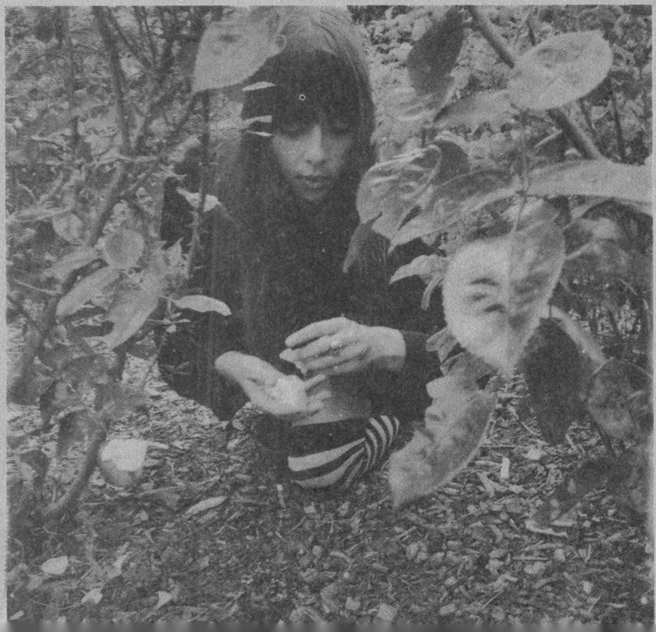

Fish, Chickpea and Chorizo Mix
Sam Belinfante

SERVES 30

a bucket of dried chickpeas
a smidgeon of salt
a few pinches of saffron
10 white-fish fillets
a drizzle of oil
an armful of onions
a bulb of garlic
some chillies
20 chorizos
a handful of ground cumin
a sprinkling of paprika
a few bay leaves
2 cinnamon sticks
2 jugs of chicken stock
a gallon of canned tomatoes
a large bowl of spinach

Pour the chickpeas into a metal bucket. Slowly drip water into the bucket until the chickpeas are covered. Leave them in silence overnight.

Drain the chickpeas quickly through a sieve, over a sink. Shake the chickpeas into a large pan and cover again with water from an elevated jug.

Add heat and bring the mixture to a vigorous boil then down to a calm simmer. Agitate for 2 hours or until the chickpeas are softened. Allow them to cool in their water.

Sprinkle the fish with a mixture of salt and saffron and put them in plastic bags. Throw a little of the mixture over your shoulder. Refrigerate for 2 hours.

Chop the onions, garlic and chillies and fling them into a pan with the oil. Cook for about 10 minutes until soft. Cut the chorizos into thumb-size pieces and toss in. Cook for a further 5 minutes.

Fold in the cumin, paprika, bay leaves and cinnamon sticks. Cook for a further 3 minutes. Rapidly pour the chicken stock and tomatoes into the pan.

Simmer for half a day.

Wash the fish fillets in cold water and lay them gently on top of the mix. Boil gently for another 10 to 15 minutes, depending on the size of the fish.

Stir in the spinach just before finishing.

Recipe inspired by Tom Kerridge and George Brecht
Recommended listening: Philip Glass, *Einstein on the Beach*, 1975

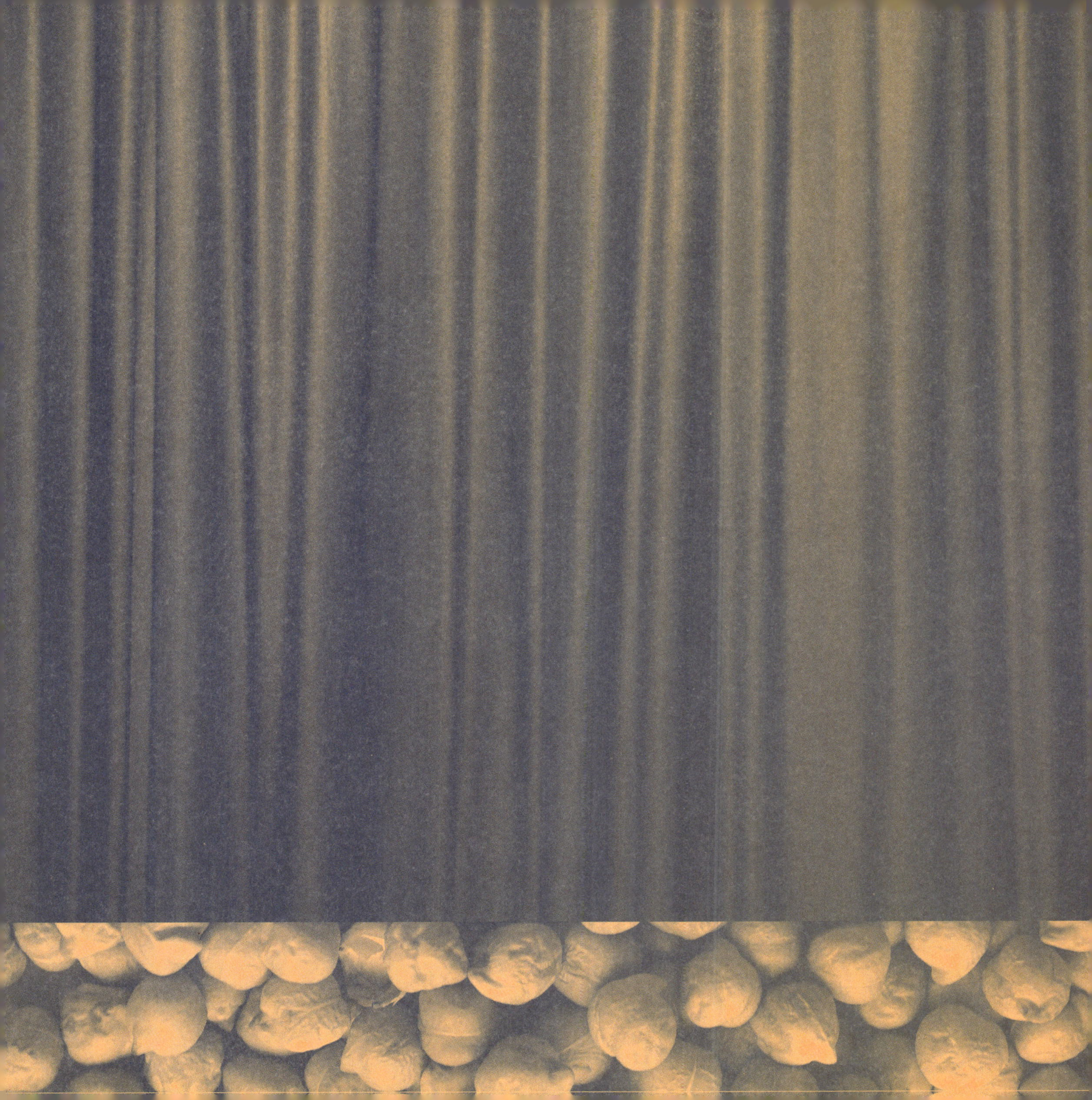

Pineapple Thai Curry
Leviathen Hendricks

PER PERSON

handful of cashews
handful of pineapple chunks
(and some juice, optional)
coconut oil
handful of broccoli spears
½ red bell pepper, deseeded and in strips
spoonful of Thai red curry paste
mouthful of coconut milk
handful of jasmine rice
bunch of Thai basil
slice of lime

Toast cashews in hot dry wok or pan, then remove and set aside.

Fry pineapple chunks on high heat till lightly browned; set aside.

Add a little coconut oil to the wok and cook broccoli and bell pepper strips, but keep them firm and not too soft; then set aside.

Add paste to empty wok and heat. Pour in coconut milk.

Add pineapple juice to taste, if desired.

Add cooked broccoli, peppers, pineapple and cashews.

Serve on top of cooked rice with Thai basil garnish and a squeeze of lime.

Adjust amounts as desired.

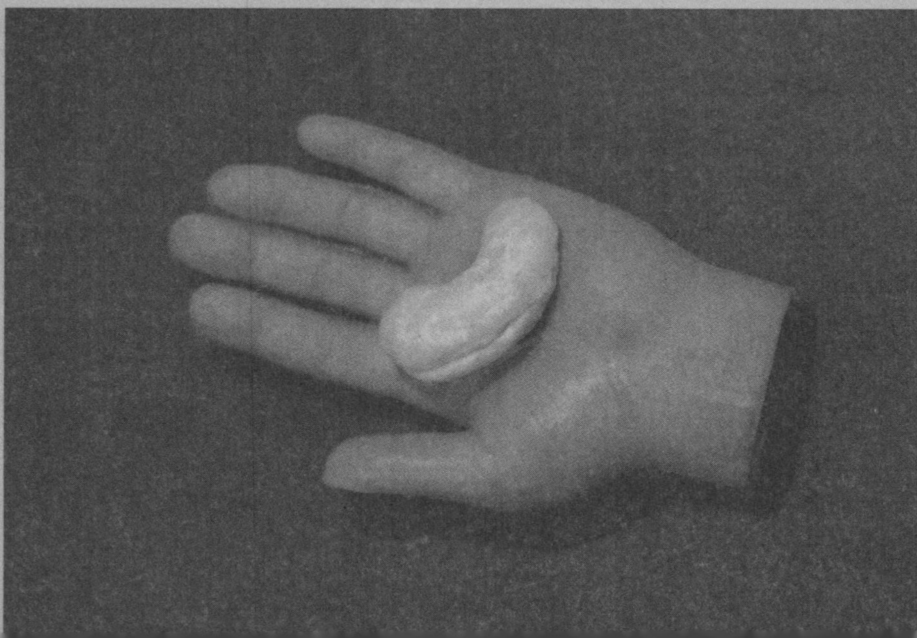

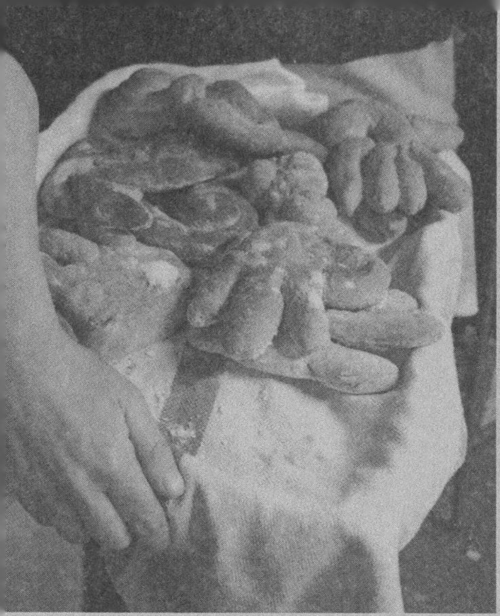

Greek Navy Bean Soup (Fasolada) The Saturday Museum: George Moustakas and Lucy Steggals

SERVES 45–50

5 kilograms white beans, medium-sized
10 celery sticks
30 carrots
10 onions
10 cloves garlic
olive oil
tomato paste
10 bay leaves
10 sprigs rosemary
3 red apples
salt
pepper
feta cheese
anchovies
olives
fresh thyme

Put the beans in a bowl, add salt and fill with water until they are completely covered. Allow them to soak overnight. The next day, drain and wash them well. Chop the celery and carrots into small pieces, chop the onions and thinly slice the garlic. Place the largest pot you can find over medium heat and add olive oil and the vegetables. Don't let the pot get too hot. Sauté for 15–20 minutes while you check your Instagram feed and post a pictures of the pot using #flowspiral. Allow the vegetables to soften. Stir occasionally. Sit on a small chair and wait. When the juices have evaporated and the vegetables have softened add the tomato paste and sauté for 1 minute while stirring. Add the beans, bay leaves, rosemary and apples (adding the apples whole will help the soup thicken). Add water and cover the pot. Simmer for 1–1.5 hours. With friends, make bread hands from a recipe on the back of a packet. Check on the soup from time to time in case a little more water is needed. About 10 minutes before the soup is done, add salt and pepper and cover. Take a spin round the kitchen on a go-kart. When ready, remove from heat and remove apples from the pot and discard them.

Ladle the soup into bowls and top with extra virgin olive oil, salt and pepper. Serve along with feta cheese, anchovies, olives, fresh thyme, bread hands and olive oil. For dessert we suggest spiralled apples and liquorice wheels.

#thesaturdaymuseum
#flowspiral

Butternut Squash and Carrot Curry
Gerald Mak, Yoojin Lee and Marta Fernàndez

SERVES 30

10 tablespoons fresh ginger, grated
30 cloves garlic, minced
10 lemons
olive oil
10 teaspoons cumin seeds
10 onions, chopped
10 teaspoons turmeric
10 teaspoons garam masala
water
5 butternut squash
40 carrots
5 cups coconut milk
black pepper

Mix the ginger and garlic with the juice of the lemons. Set aside.

Pour about 500 millilitres of olive oil into a pan at medium heat. Once the olive oil is hot add the cumin seeds.

When the cumin seeds have stopped simmering add the chopped onion, garlic/ginger paste, turmeric, garam masala, and about 500 millilitres of water. Let the mixture simmer at a low heat for 5 minutes. Peel and cube the butternut squash and carrots and add to the pan with the coconut milk. Let simmer at a low heat until the butternut squash and carrots are soft (about 20–30 minutes). Remove from heat and add 4 pinches of black pepper.

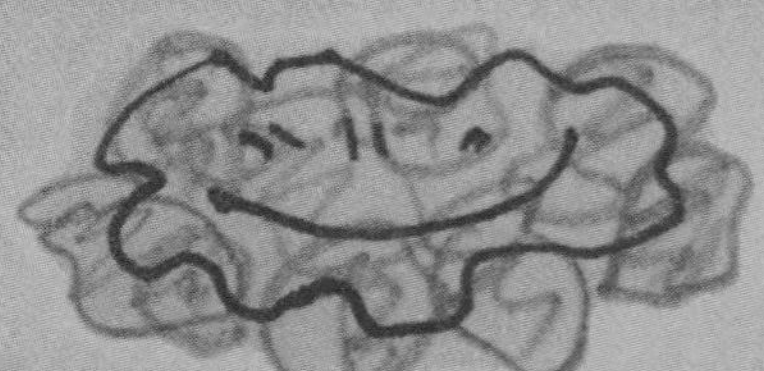

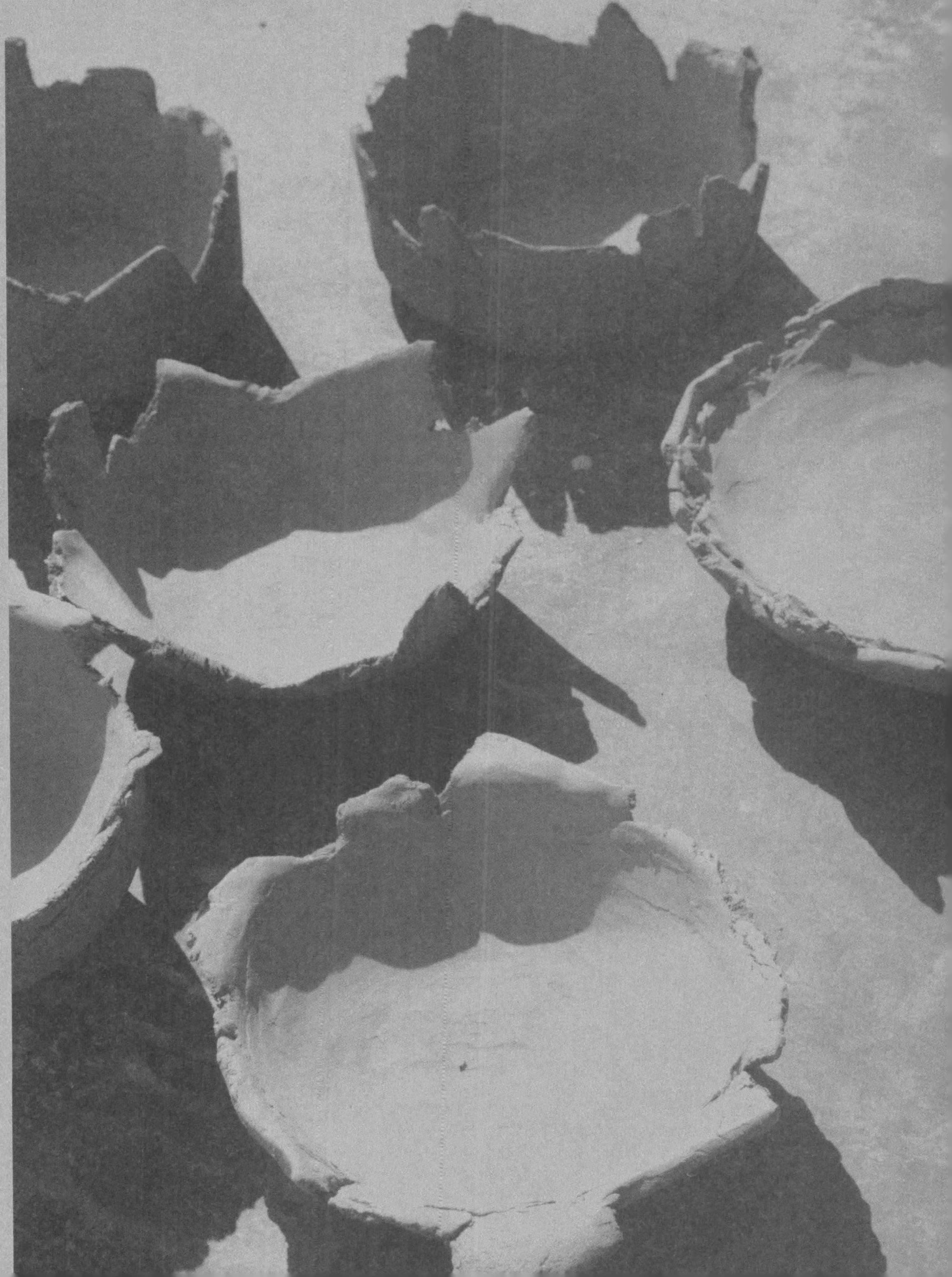

Fricandó
Jordi Canals

SERVES 4

FOR THE FRICANDÓ
300 grams brisket beef
(you can use Quorn and beans for a vegetarian option)
salt
pepper
flour
olive oil
1 onion, chopped
2 garlic cloves, minced
1 big spoonful tomato paste
4 bay leaves
½ glass white wine
2 glasses water
(with some vegetable stock)
1 box mushrooms
(shiitake, oyster, or a mix)
250 grams green peas

FOR LA PICADA
22 grams toasted almonds without salt
½ cup parsley
20 grams croutons

This is a recipe inspired from my land, Catalonia—inspired because the ingredients are not the same, but the idea is. We call it *fricandó*. Its secret is the *sofregit*, a nonexistent word in English that refers to the main base of many Spanish recipes.

FRICANDÓ

1 Clean the brisket of any nerves or tendons and cut into chunks.

2 Season the meat with salt and pepper, cover in flour.

3 Add a thin layer of oil to a large pot. Turn the heat up, being careful not to burn the oil.

4 When the oil is really hot, brown the meat on both sides, just a few seconds for each side. Remove the meat from the pot; set aside.

5 Add the onion and garlic to the same pot and oil. Turn the heat down, stirring from time to time.

6 When the onion is golden, sieve in flour and mix to create a consistent paste.

7 Add the tomato paste and bay leaves and keep mixing for about two minutes.

8 Add the white wine and raise the heat, letting the alcohol evaporate.

9 Add the meat and any juices it released.

10 Add the water with some vegetable stock, bring to boil, and simmer until the liquid has reduced by half.

11 Cover the pot and simmer for about two hours, stirring every now and then. (An hour is usually enough, but brisket is tougher than other cuts of meat.)

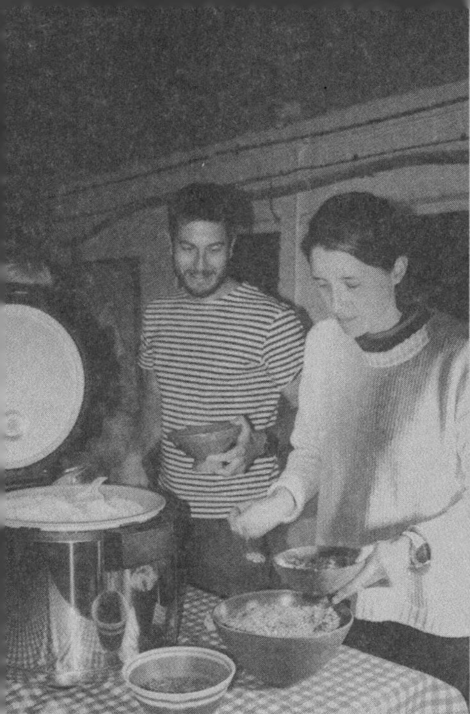

12 Add the mushrooms and cook for 30 minutes; add the peas in the last 5 minutes.

13 Once the meat is tender, remove it from the pot and shred it.

14 Put the meat back and check the stew. Add more salt if needed.

LA PICADA

A blender is going to simplify your life, otherwise use a mortar. Blend all ingredients together. Add the picada when serving the *fricandó*, with basmati or long-grain rice as a side. *El fricandó és a taula, bon profit.*

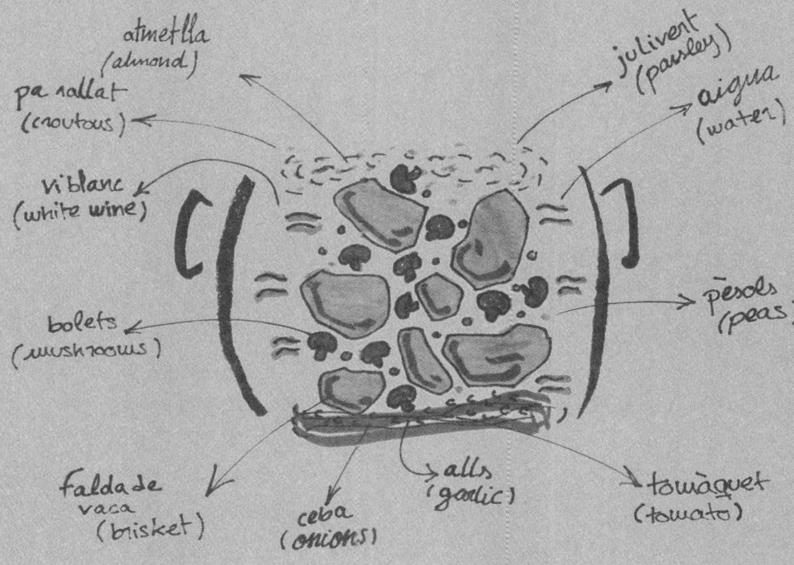

Aromatic Chicken Curry
Ambra Medda and Edward Barber

SERVES 4

8–10 boneless, skinless chicken thighs
1 tablespoon natural yogurt
1 teaspoon garam masala
1 teaspoon ground cumin
1 teaspoon ground coriander
1 teaspoon salt
large chunk of ginger
4 small green chillies
5 tablespoons corn
or peanut oil and ghee
1 large red chilli
1 stick cinnamon
1 teaspoon mustard seeds
2 medium-sized onions, finely chopped
medium bunch of coriander
500 grams cherry tomatoes, chopped
5 cloves garlic, crushed or grated
1 teaspoon ground cumin
2 teaspoon turmeric powder
2 teaspoon coriander seeds, crushed
2 teaspoon ground coriander
cardamom seeds from at least 12 pods
salt
fresh curry leaves, chopped

MARINADE

Chop the chicken into bite-size pieces. Mix together yogurt, garam masala, ground cumin, ground coriander and salt thoroughly, coat chicken pieces, cover and refrigerate for 12 hours.

GINGER-CHILLI PASTE

Scrape the ginger with a teaspoon to remove the skin and chop the green chillies into small pieces. Put the ginger and chillies into a blender with a dash of water. Blend into a fine paste and set aside.

CURRY

In a large heavy bottomed pan, heat oil and ghee. When hot, add the red chilli and cinnamon. Add the mustard seeds, cook until they start to pop. Add the onions and coriander stalks and let them cook for 6–8 minutes, stirring regularly until golden. Add the cherry tomatoes, garlic, ground cumin, turmeric powder, coriander seeds, ground coriander, 1 tablespoon of the ginger-chilli paste, cardamom seeds and salt. Let the sauce cook for 10 minutes, stirring regularly. Add the marinated chicken. Put the lid on and cook for 30 minutes, stirring occasionally. Finally add the curry leaves and a large handful of chopped coriander leaves and serve with basmati rice, dal and bread.

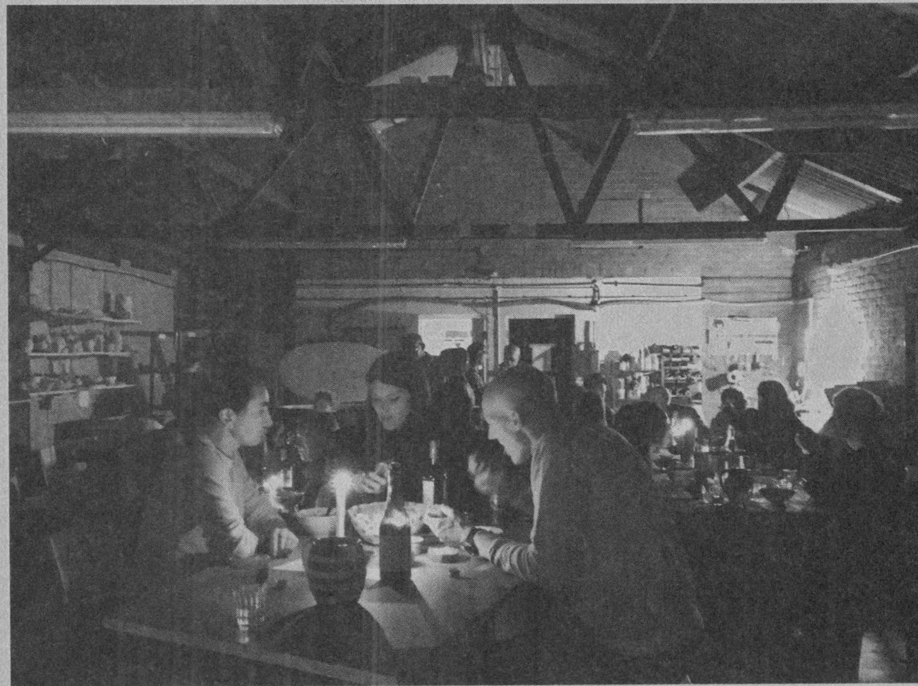

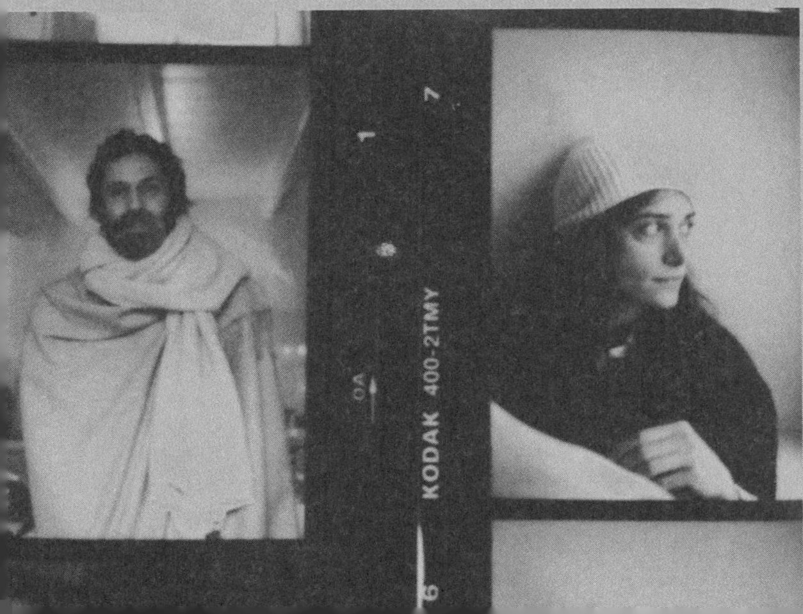
KODAK 400-2TMY

A Theme and Variation on Tomatoes and Beans
Milan Tarascas and Ellie Wang

SERVES 30

FOR THE SALSA
20 white onions
10 red peppers
10 yellow peppers
10 bulbs garlic
paprika
ground cumin
ground cinnamon
cayenne pepper
1 tube tomato purée
20 cans chopped tomatoes
5 kilograms fresh tomatoes

FOR THE REFRIED BEANS
40 red onions
20 green peppers
10 bulbs garlic
cube of vegetable stock
20 400-gram cans kidney beans
paprika

FOR THE CHILLI OIL
500 grams dried chilli flakes
500 grams dried crispy onions
salt
sugar
vegetable oil

FOR THE SOUR CREAM AND CHIVE
3 handfuls of chives
2 kilograms sour cream

FOR THE TORTILLAS
12 kilograms flour
cumin seeds
vegetable oil

FOR THE GUACAMOLE
1 bulb garlic
12 avocados
juice from 2 lemons
paprika

SALSA

Finely slice the onions, peppers and garlic and sauté in olive oil until they start to brown. Add the spices and tomato purée and cook until fragrant. Add tomatoes, canned and fresh, and cook uncovered for 10 minutes on a high heat. Lower the heat and simmer for 50 minutes with the lid on. Season to taste.

REFRIED BEANS

Dice the onions, peppers and garlic and sauté in vegetable oil until they start to brown. Dissolve vegetable-stock cube in a cup of water and add to the pan with drained kidney beans. Add two more cups of water and leave to simmer until beans become soft. Roughly mash the mix, keeping some of the texture. Serve with a sprinkle of paprika.

CHILLI OIL

Mix chilli flakes and crispy onions in a large bowl. Add some salt and sugar. Heat oil in a pan. To test the temperature of the oil, drop a couple chilli flakes in – when they sizzle, take the pan off the heat (make sure the oil isn't too hot or the chilli flakes will burn) then pour oil over chilli-onion mix. Leave to sit until ready to serve.

SOUR CREAM AND CHIVE

Dice chives, and in a large bowl mix them with sour cream. Season lightly with salt and pepper and garnish with fresh parsley.

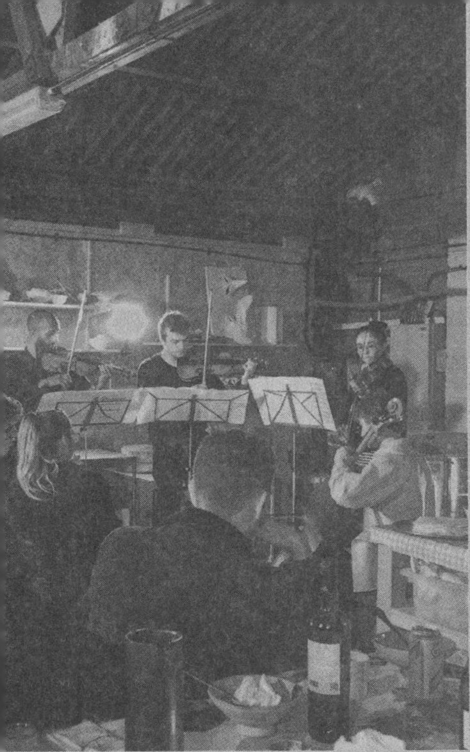

TORTILLAS

To make the dough, mix the cumin seeds into the flour. Gradually add water and a small amount of oil. Knead until dough forms. Wrap in cling film and leave to rest for 30 minutes. Once the dough has rested, divide it into portions slightly smaller than a tennis ball. Roll into a circle, and fry both sides in a hot dry pan. Stack the finished tortillas and cover with foil. Reheat in oven just before serving.

GUACAMOLE

Finely chop garlic and mix with avocados in a large bowl, seasoning and mashing thoroughly. Top with lemon juice and paprika.

SOUNDTRACK
Handel, Sarabande
Mussorgsky, *Night on Bald Mountain*
Tchaikovsky, String Quartet No. 1 in D, Movement 2 (Andante Cantabile)

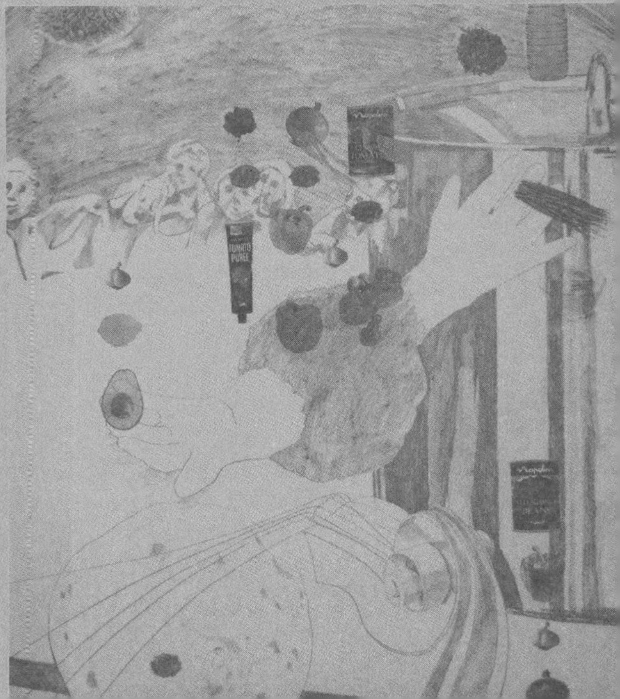

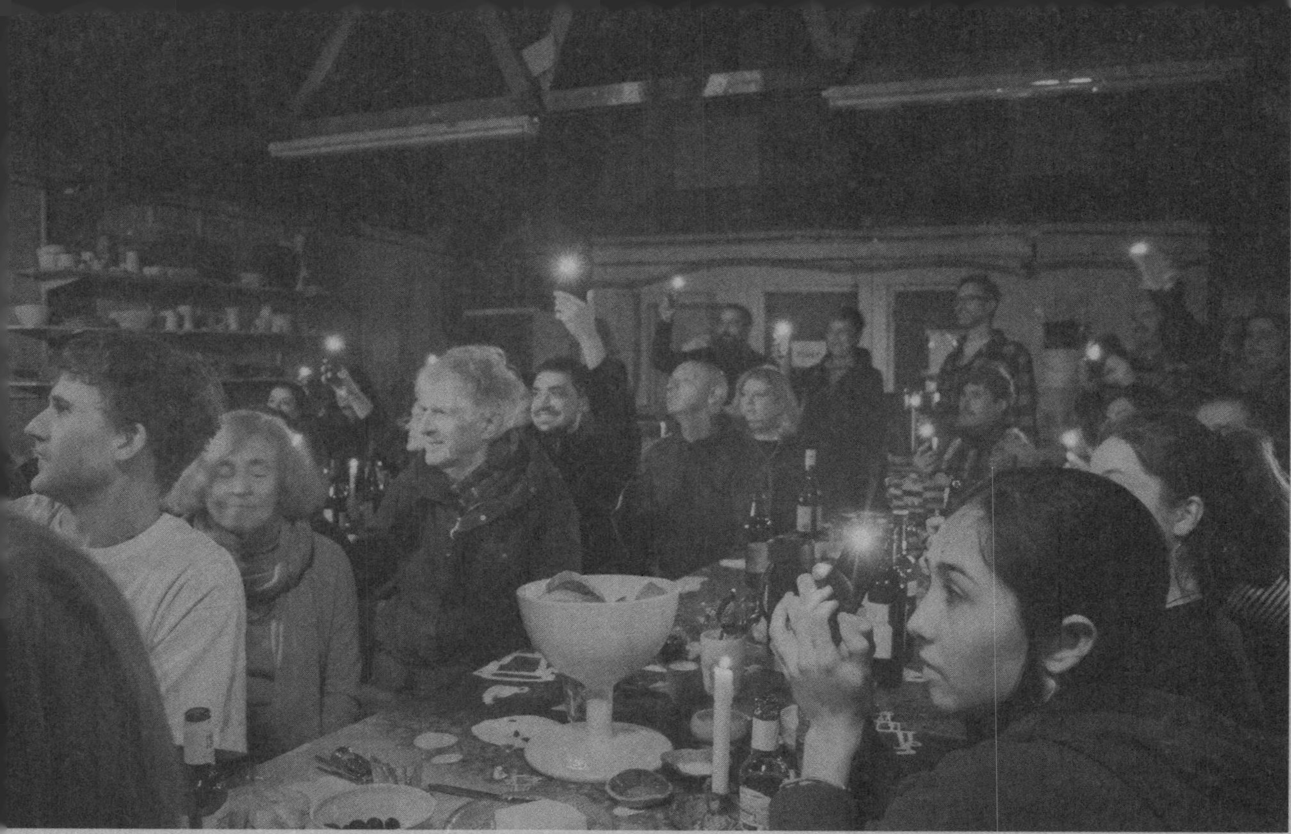

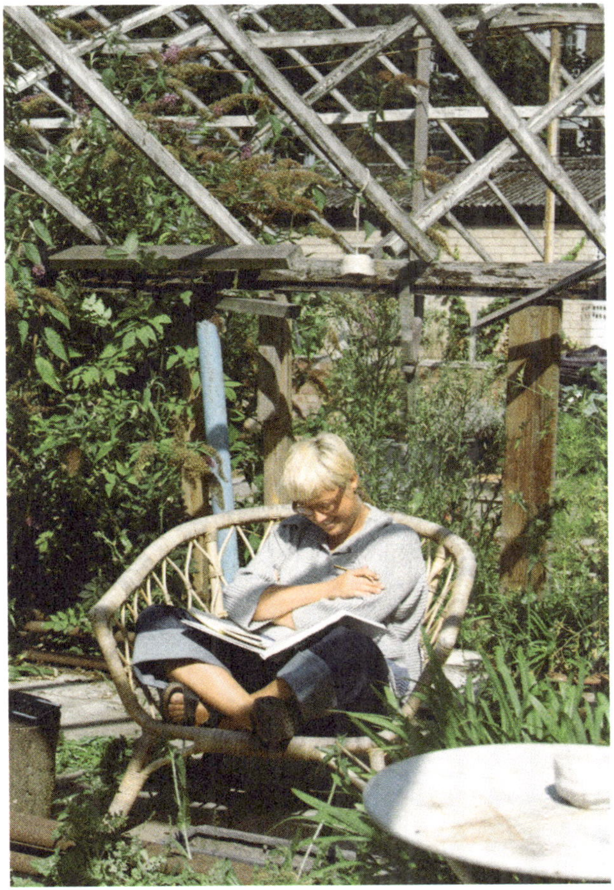

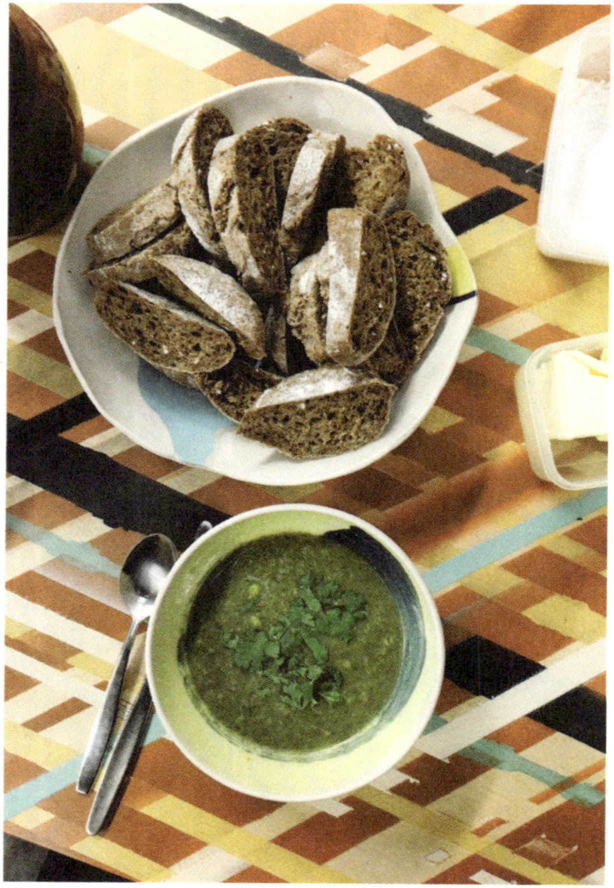

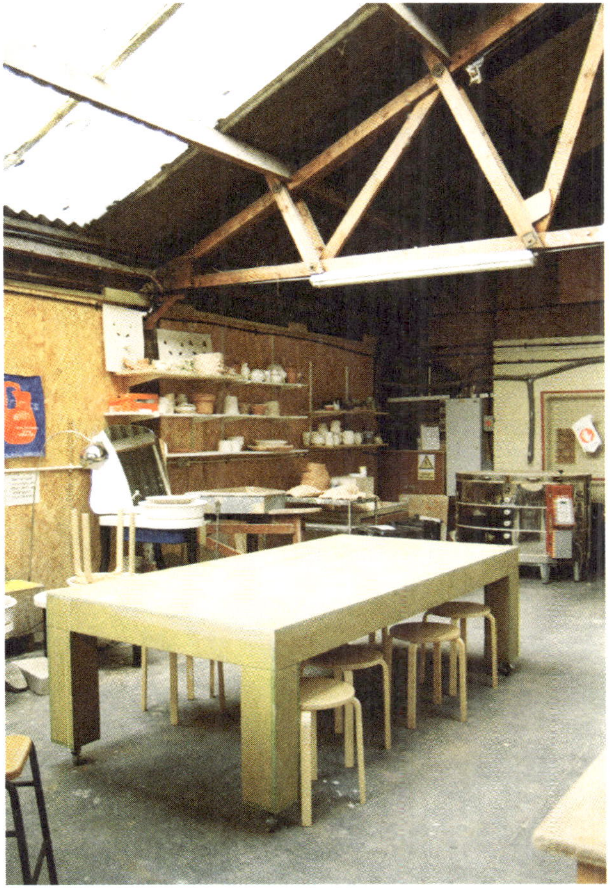

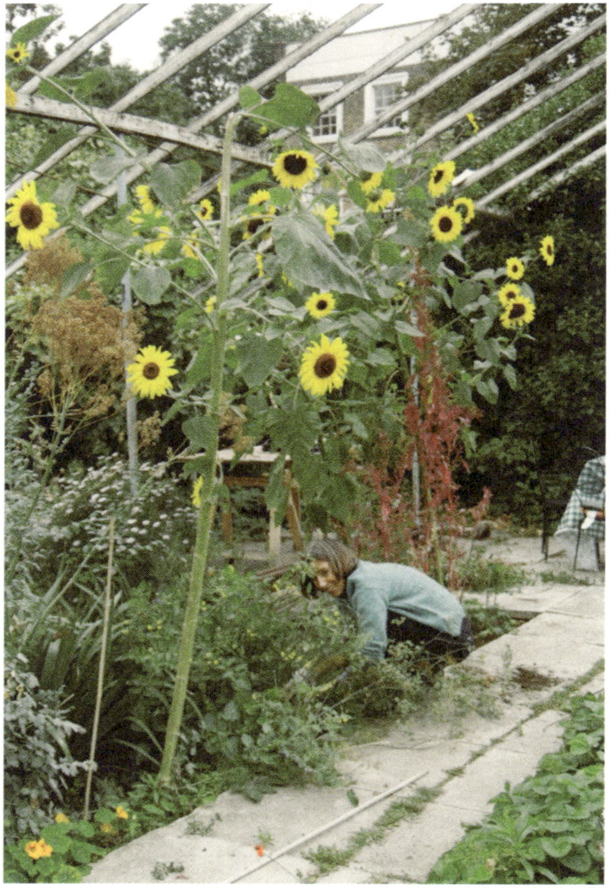

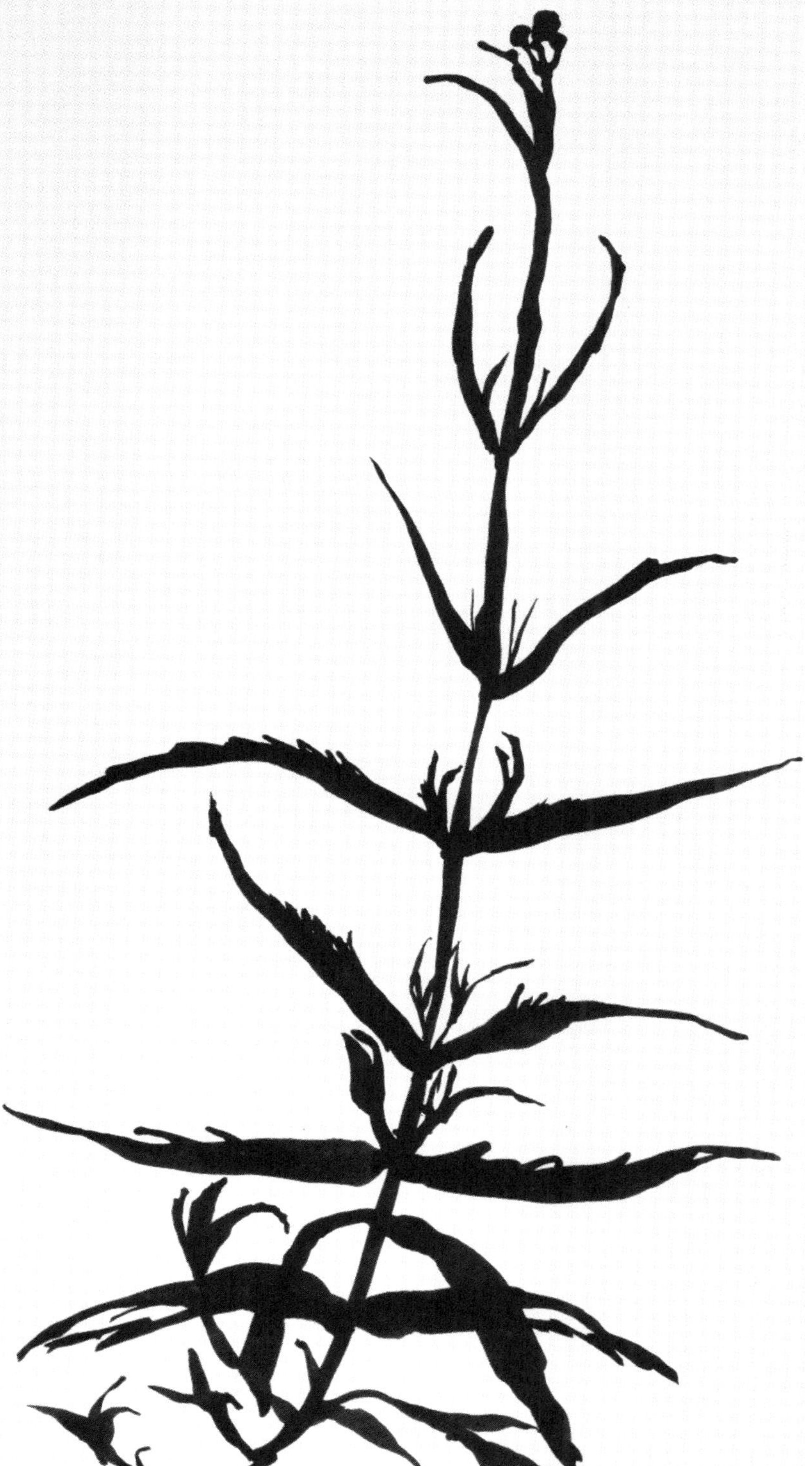

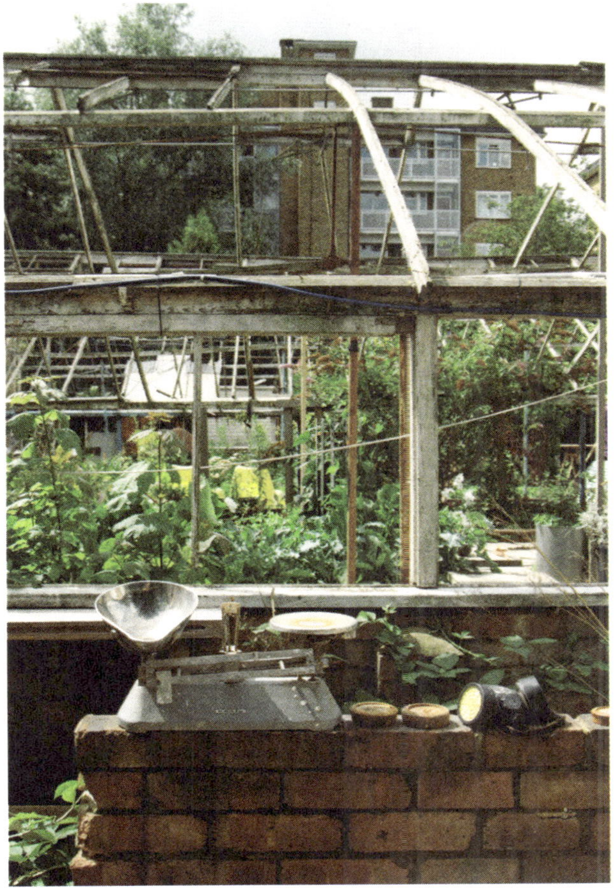

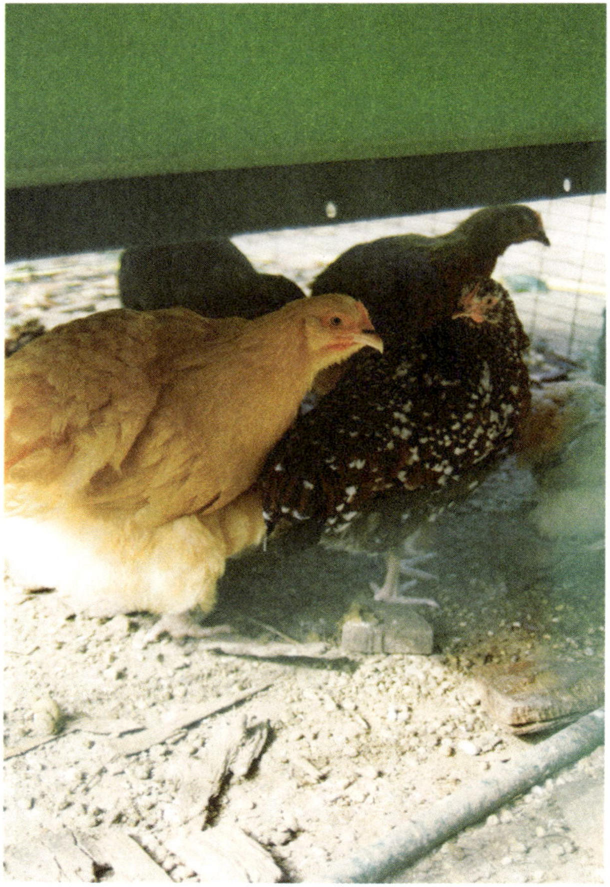

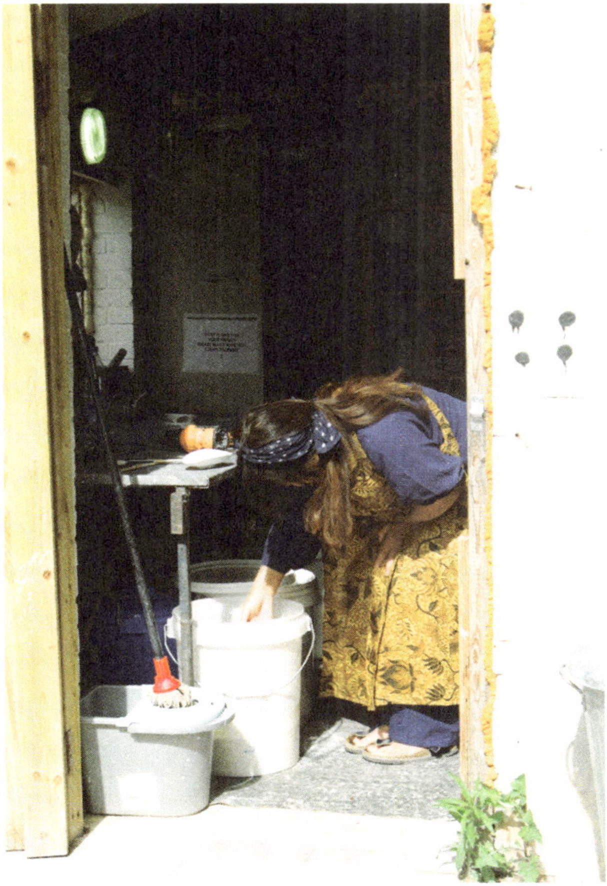

Growing Together
Francesca Astesani

> Paradise haunts gardens, and some gardens are paradises. Mine is one of them.
> — Derek Jarman

As I sit here in front of my screen, gathering thoughts on Rochester Square's garden, I realise that they share something, my text and the garden. They are both at the beginning of a process, and as I am looking for the words to formulate the present and especially the future of this garden, I can see how these lines of text will be attempting to plough the soil of its wishes. Except they are also opposites, my text and the garden: one, a blank luminous page staring passively at me, the other, a messy, dense and beautiful plot of urban nature evolving wildly through its own force. The garden of Rochester Square, after being abandoned for more than two decades, has in the last few years started a long process of restoring its planting facilities and opening up to the community in line with its history and the London Squares Preservation Act of 1931, which defines the square as a site for relaxation and recreational activities.

The currently run-down conservatories at the centre of the square, whose only standing remains are ruined wooden structures, testify to the site's origin as a plant nursery in the first half of the nineteenth century. From the early 1920s to the late 1980s, the nursery was owned by Strouds, a film-props company that specialised in palm trees, but when the company went out of business the square was abandoned for a long period, leaving the nurseries to ruin. There is a kind of beauty in the connection between the history of the square, once the home to a business providing exotic plants for an industry that fabricates dreams, and its present as a site of a dream: to transform this piece of urban London into a green space for the commons.

However, the future of this garden can only be fully understood in relation to the other main activities taking place at Rochester Square: its ceramic production and the projects around food. A creative 'earth cycle' moulds the activities of the square.

This image makes me think not only that Rochester Square is a real site with a real garden in the process of being shaped and defined, but also that the garden is one of the key meta-narratives behind the overall project. A garden, as we learn from Michel Foucault, is a symbolically charged place, at once separated and connected to the outside world, a classic example of what the French philosopher defined as 'heterotopia'. In contrast to utopias, which do not exist, heterotopias are real places that allow the shifting of hierarchies and temporalities of the 'real' world, and are defined by their own set of symbolic structures. In synergistic gardening, plants are combined so that they can defend and nurture each other, creating a self-supportive system that doesn't need external agents to thrive. I see a clear affinity between this gardening method and philosophy and the holistic image of the square's activities.

The garden is today a combination of invasive plants, cultivated vegetable gardens and wildflower beds. This blending allows for a nonhierarchical cohabiting of different kinds of flora, and creates a sense of unkempt, romantic beauty. Invasive species creep up through the square's largely cemented pavement with a resilience that suggests a certain form of resistance – towards the urban density of the surroundings as well as a rationalised, man-controlled image of nature. This tension between order and wilderness expresses beautifully the idea of the garden as a site of constant negotiation between order and complexity, form and process and ultimately culture and nature. The coexistence of these oppositions is precious when trying to ontologically define what a garden is, alongside its intrinsic dependence on human care. In light of these considerations, it will be important to preserve this tension between design (cultivated, landscaped parts) and emergence (wild and invasive plants) in the future to allow the garden to speak a nuanced language composed of a diversity of resonances and symbolic orders.

Art also plays a crucial role in the image of this future garden, and the tension between formal order and nature's complexity is explored in a recent art commission by Danish artist Tue Greenfort, whose multidisciplinary practice conceptually addresses the negotiation between nature and culture against the background of today's environmental challenges and economic structures. In his work for Rochester Square, which I happened to curate, Greenfort produced five large-scale reliefs in clay inspired by the presence of invasive plants and their connection to colonial narratives. The idea for the project started from the story of Japanese knotweed, an invasive species that was being professionally eradicated from the square. The plant, originally imported from Japan at the height of power of the British Empire, carries a narrative of domination and rebellion. Once imported, the weed spread violently, and the threat its roots pose to buildings and other human infrastructure has gained it a reputation as Britain's most dangerous plant.

A number of other art commissions, all made in clay, are already present around the garden: *Green Sculpture* is a metaphorical and physical multifunctional area, part sculpture, part classroom, part bench, designed by Jake Fisk during his residency with Slade School of Fine Arts. A group of MA students from Westminster University collaborated with local architectural firm Piercy&Company to build *Pizza Oven*, a functioning oven made of clay, which is regularly used during the square's rituals of communal eating. *Shifting*, by Gerald Mak, is a site-specific work for the entrance of the ceramic facilities composed of 204 bespoke tiles in a variety of natural tones.

Most of these works play with the dynamics between form and function, shying away from pure aesthetics. It is perhaps already clear that Rochester Square, amongst other garden-things, also wishes to reinterpret the idea of a sculpture garden, incorporating art into its premises as a way to engage with its production facilities and natural surroundings rather than present art as an object purely for the sake of contemplation. For this garden dreams to be more than a place for aesthetic bliss, to be a green, active space for a community to get together through the simple but powerful tools of making (and growing) things together.

From creating objects out of clay to growing plants, from cooking and sharing a meal to artistic production, Rochester Square is first and foremost a space for the community, a creative engine for people to connect via a different route. Through this focus on making and sharing, Rochester Square pushes forward its own model of reconnecting humans to each other and to natural cycles at different scales. It is a model where plants, flowers, humans and art act together as synergistic forces, as in a thriving garden. Not to forget the seven hens living in the henhouse at the back of the warehouse. They are still young, I am told, so only one precious egg is presently collected every day, but just like the other ideas and seeds planted in this soil, they will eventually grow to full potential. From my desk, on a grey winter day in my home in Copenhagen, I can already savour the summer day I will be eating an omelette with salad from the garden, on a clay plate, with a group of others – perhaps during a break from communal gardening time.

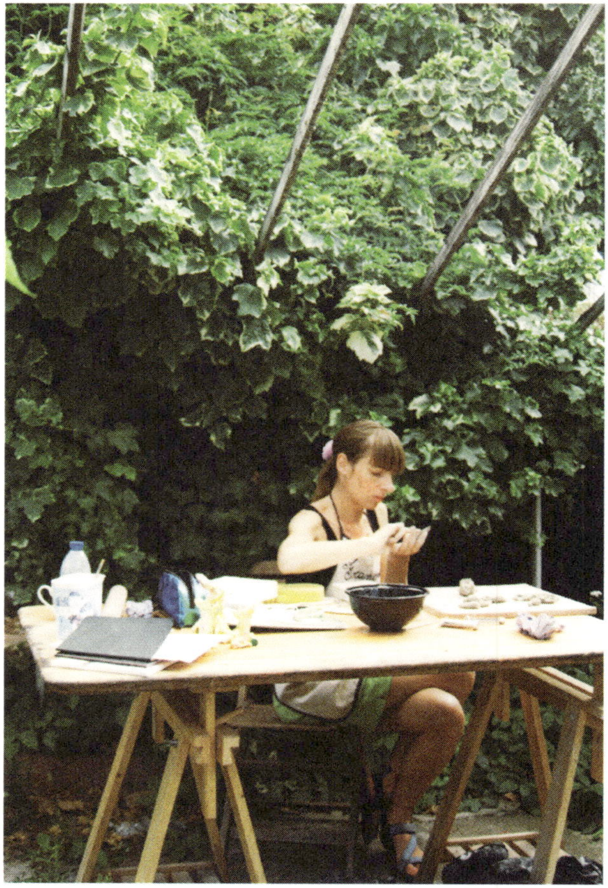

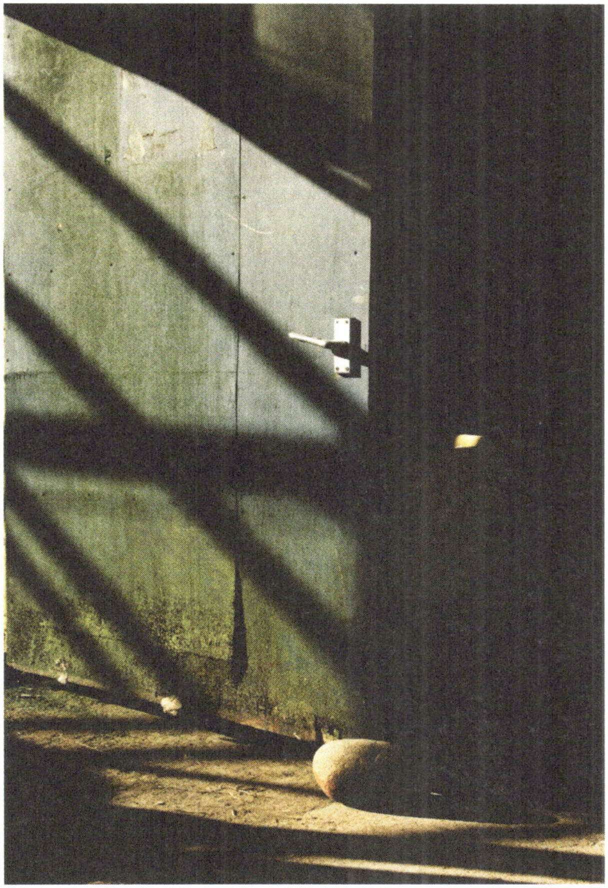

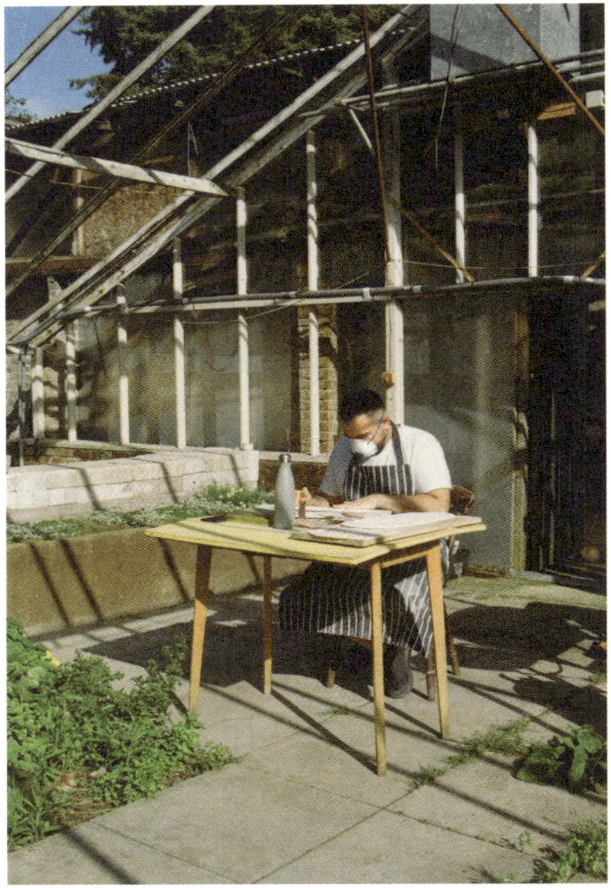

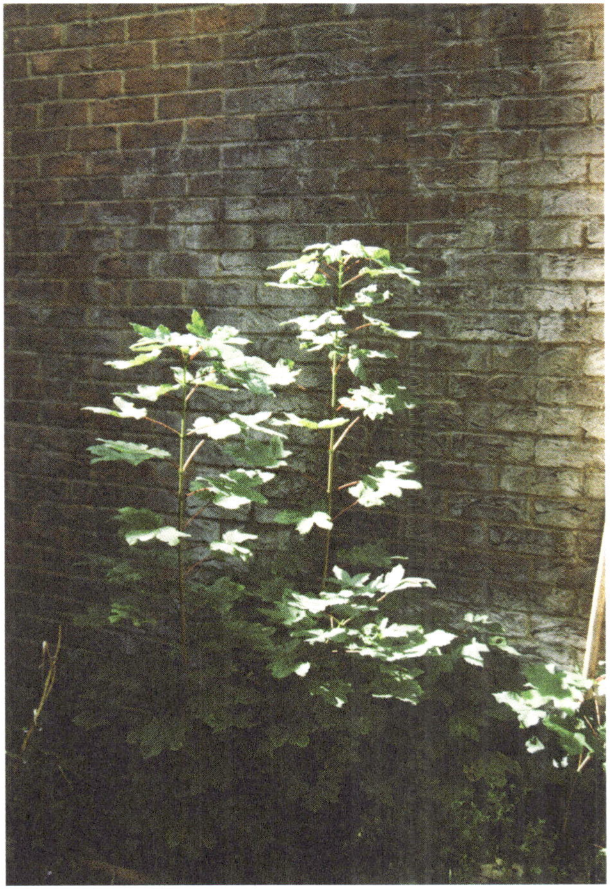

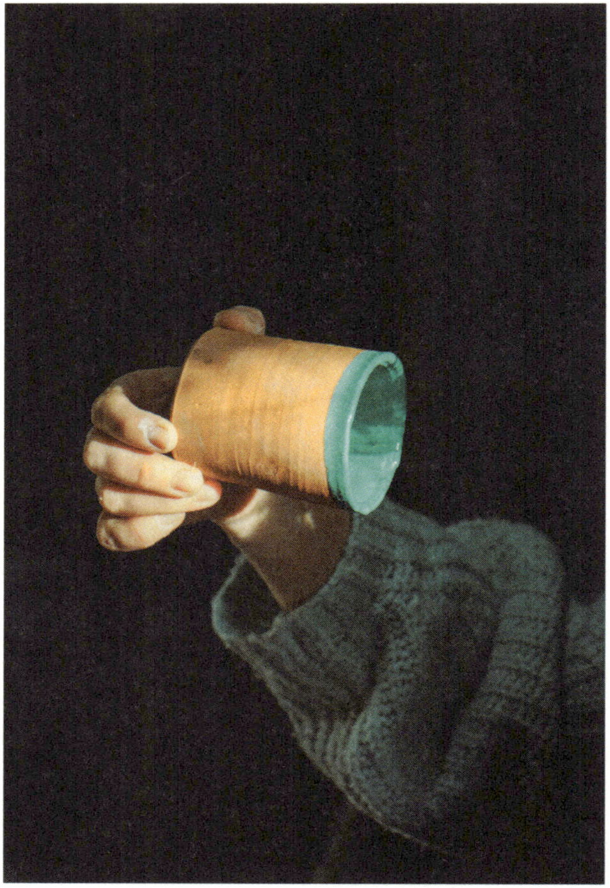

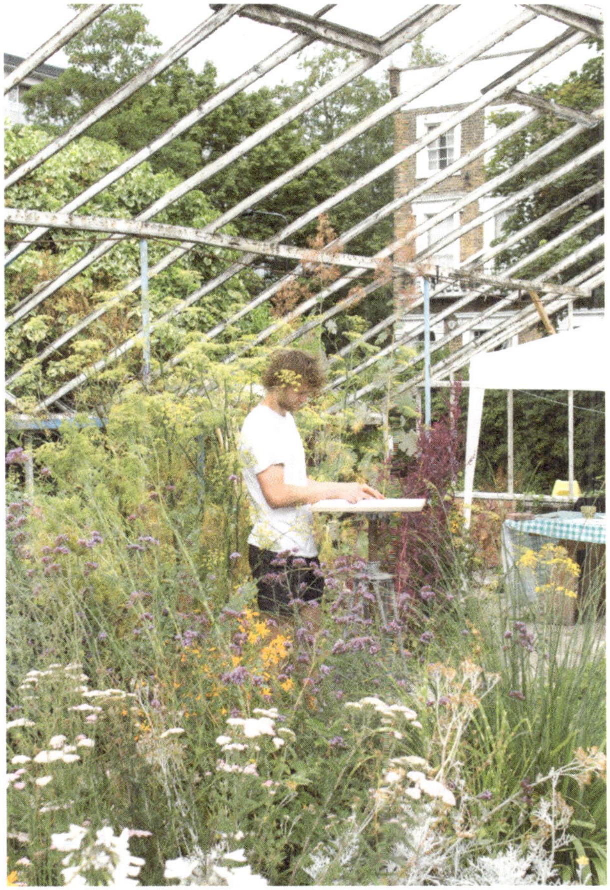

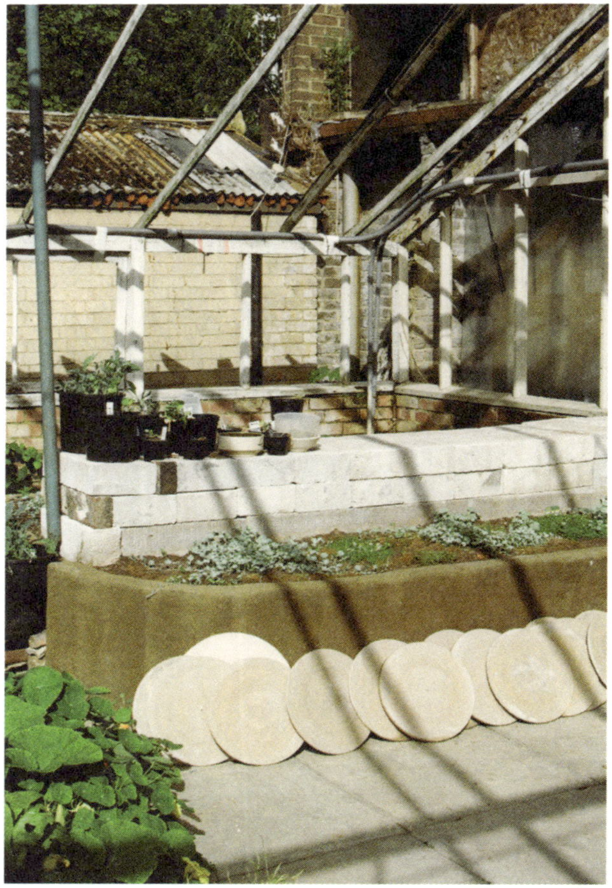

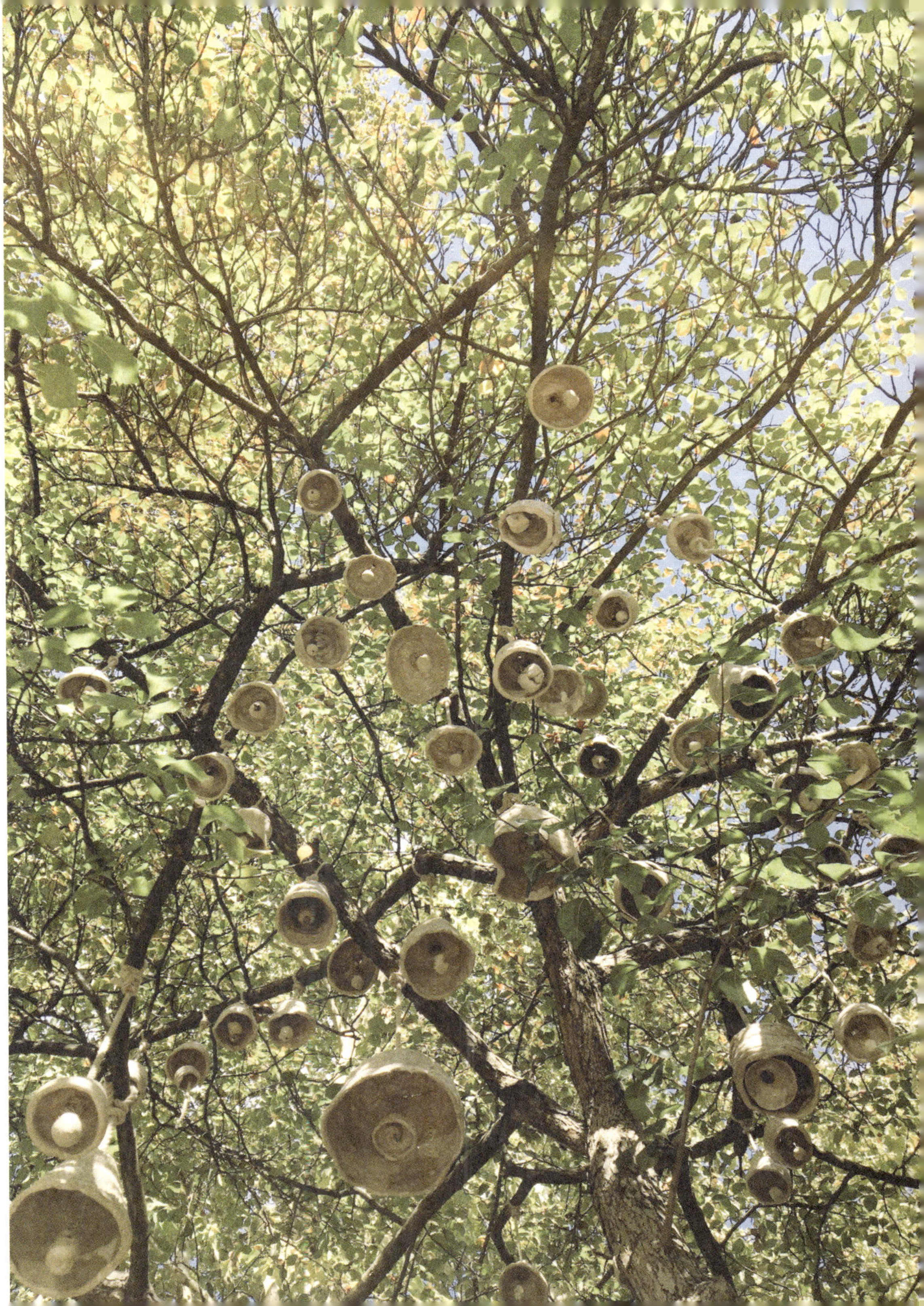

Marijke Keyser, 2018

SLADE SCHOOL OF FINE ART RESIDENCY — Since 2017, Rochester Square has been collaborating with the Slade School of Fine Art, a partnership that supports a transdisciplinary group of undergraduate and graduate students. The project has both practical and technical aims, with a focus on research and development via public engagement opportunities. With the support of Rochester Square, the students can make their own artworks, organise public workshops and events and join the square's collaborative community.

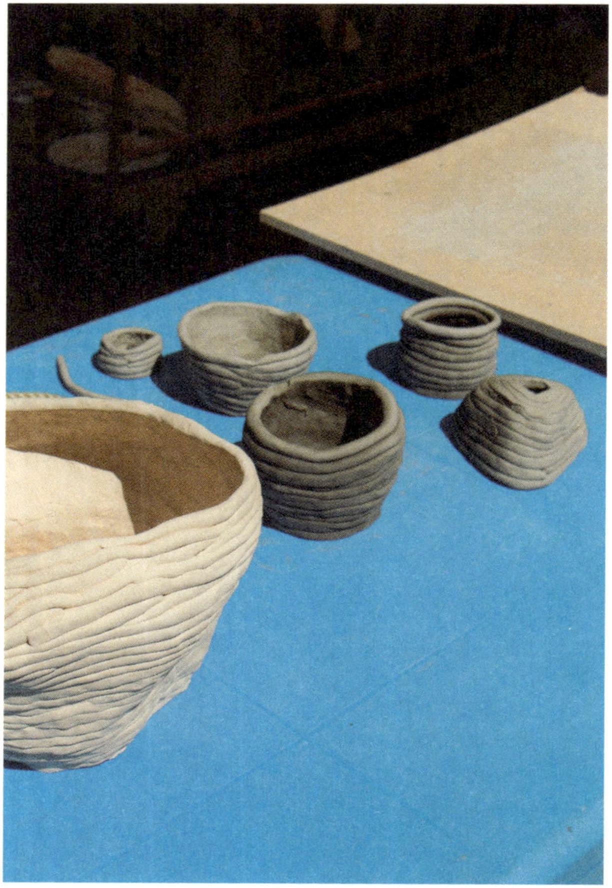

Marijke Keyser, 2018

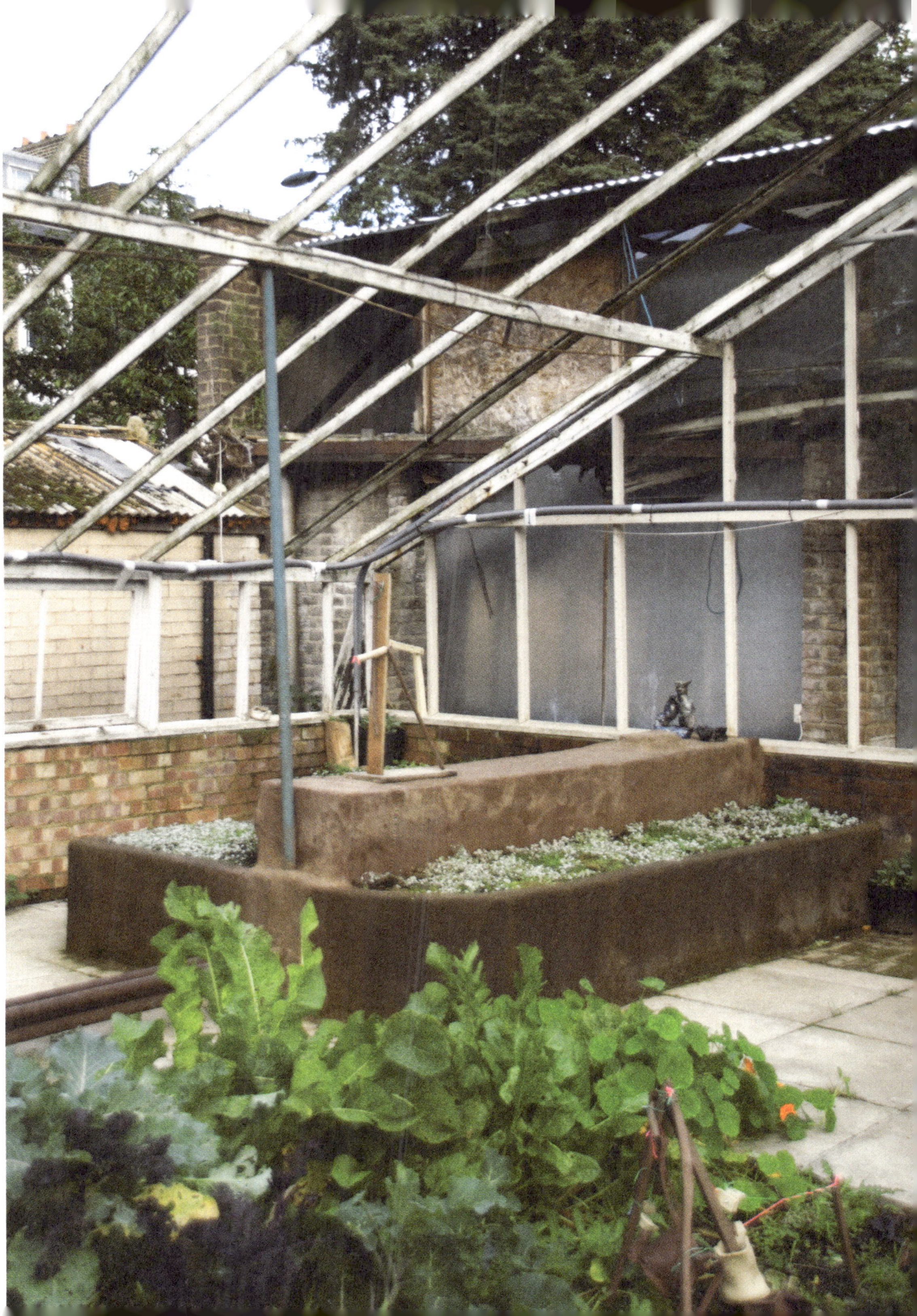

Jake Fisk, 2019

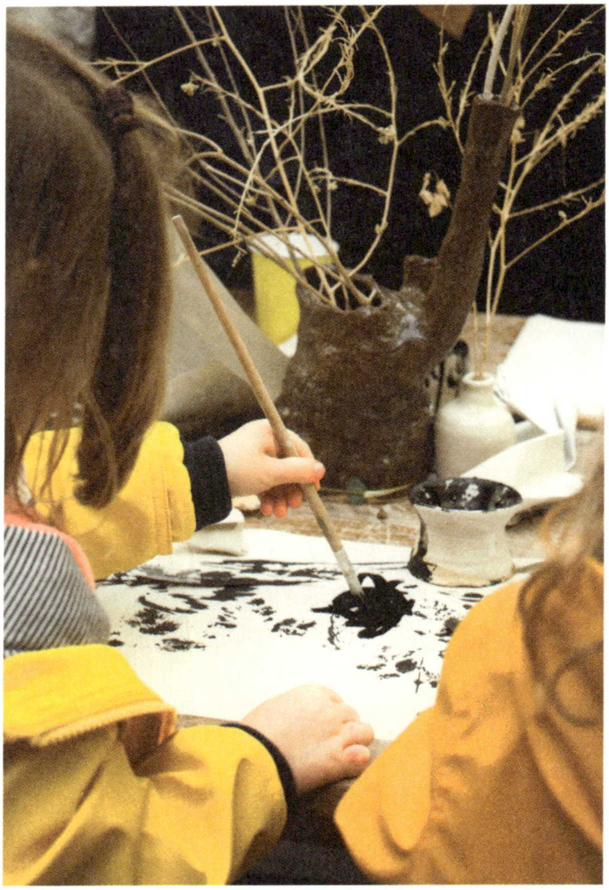

Jake Fisk, 2019

Ishwari Bhalerao and Leonie Rousham, 2019

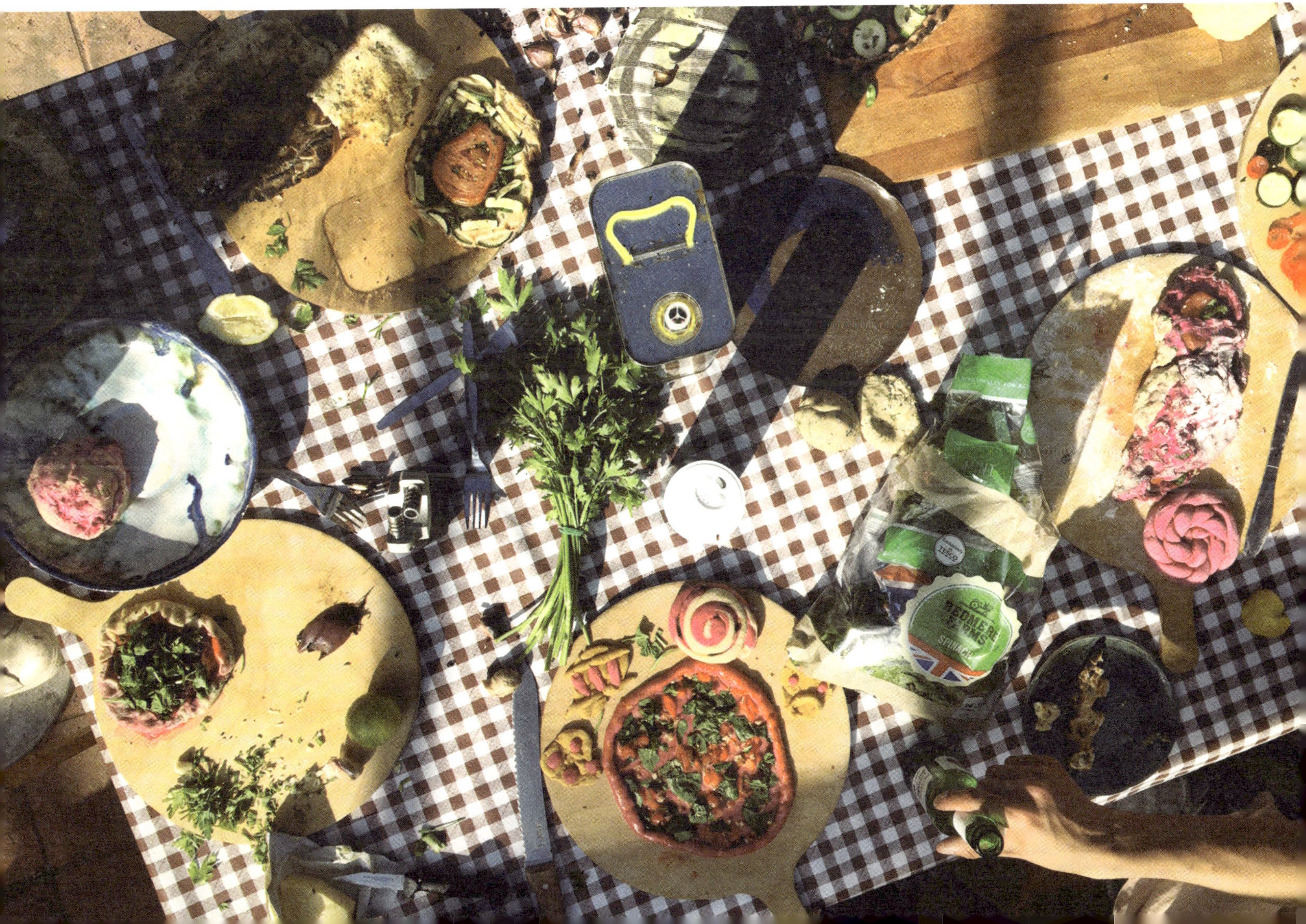

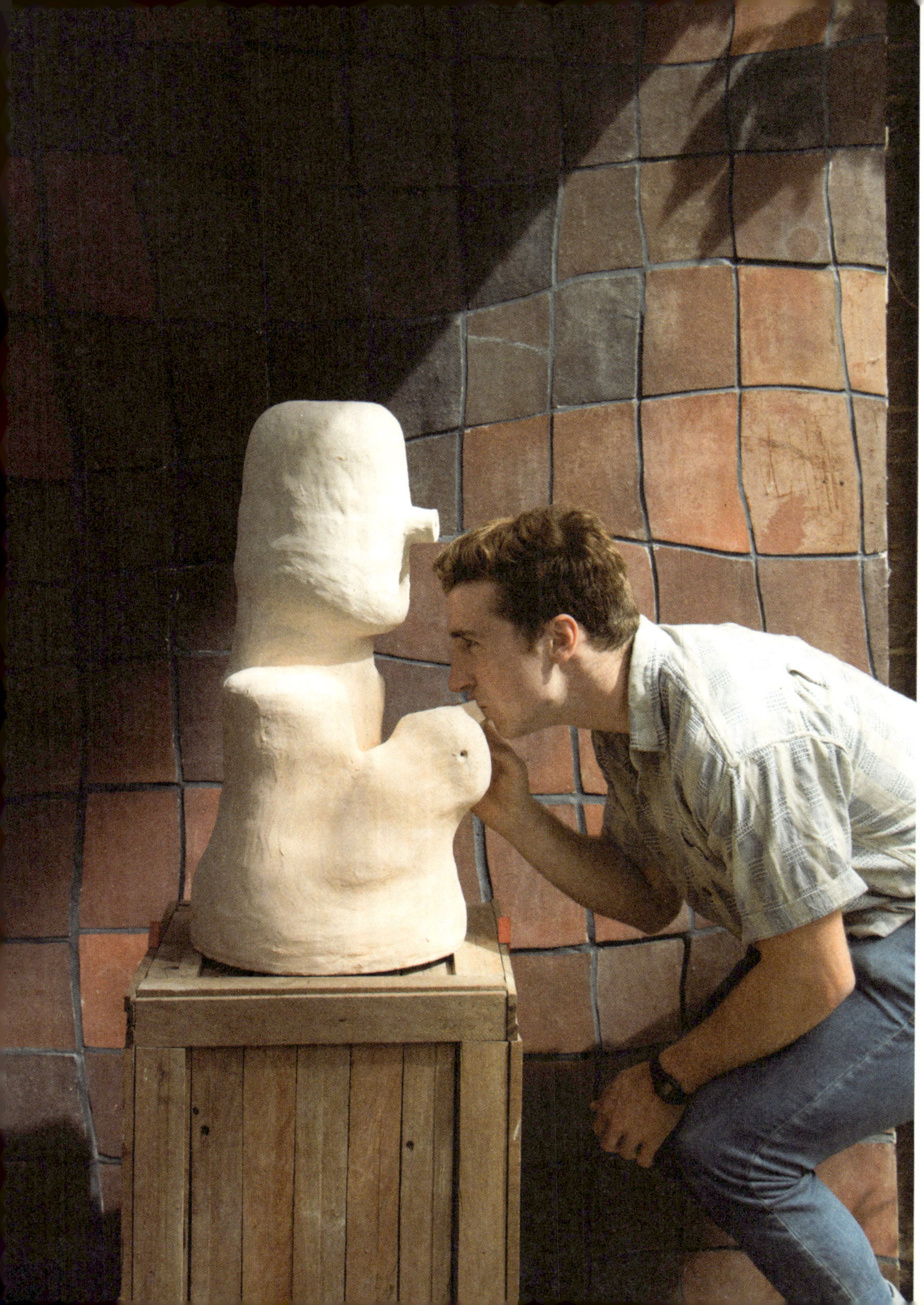

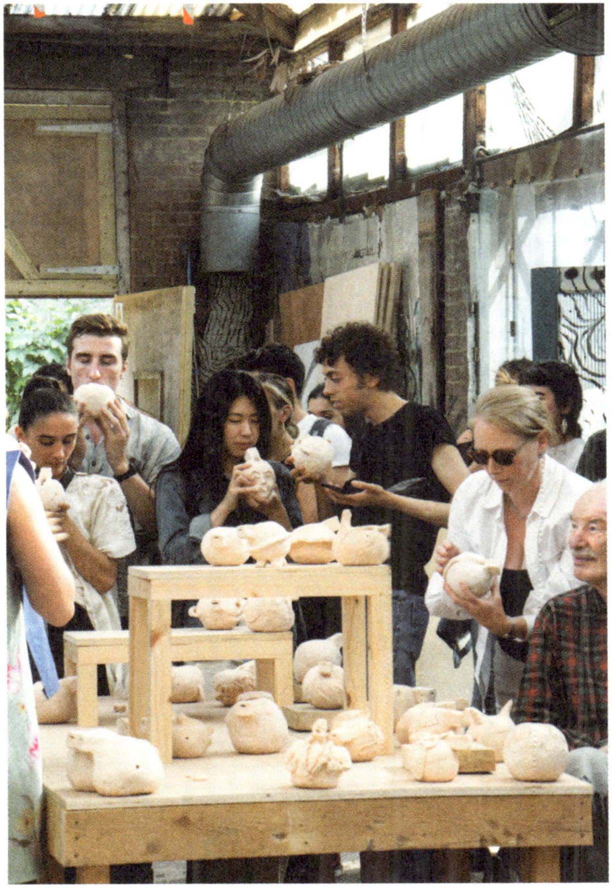

Milan Tarascas, 2018

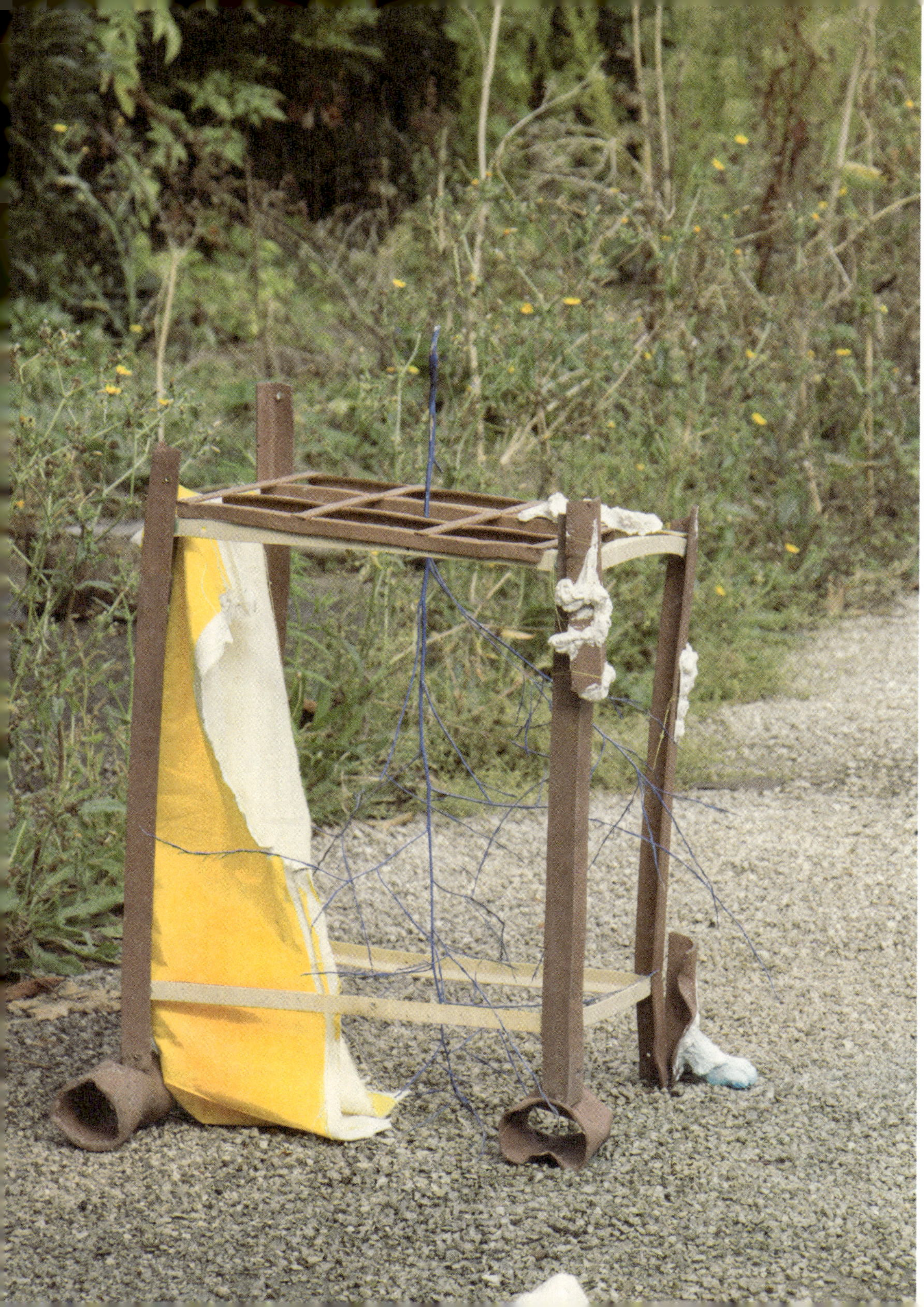

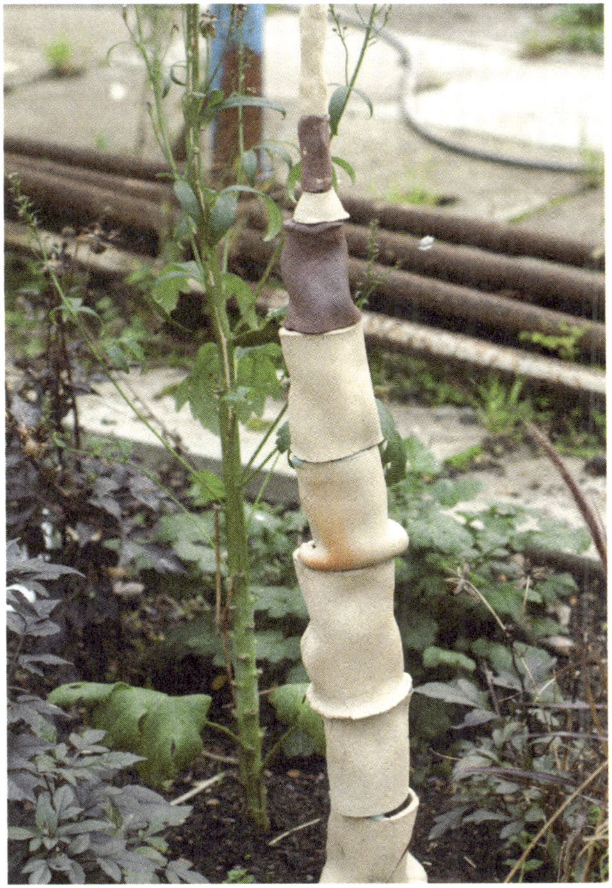

Ryan Orme, 2019

SHIFTING — In 2017, artist Gerald Mak designed a site-specific project for the entrance of Rochester Square. The piece is composed of 204 bespoke tiles with a variety of natural tones achieved by mixing different ratios of terracotta, black clay and London clay. He used clay excavated on-site to create a relationship to the original brick building that is part of Rochester Square.

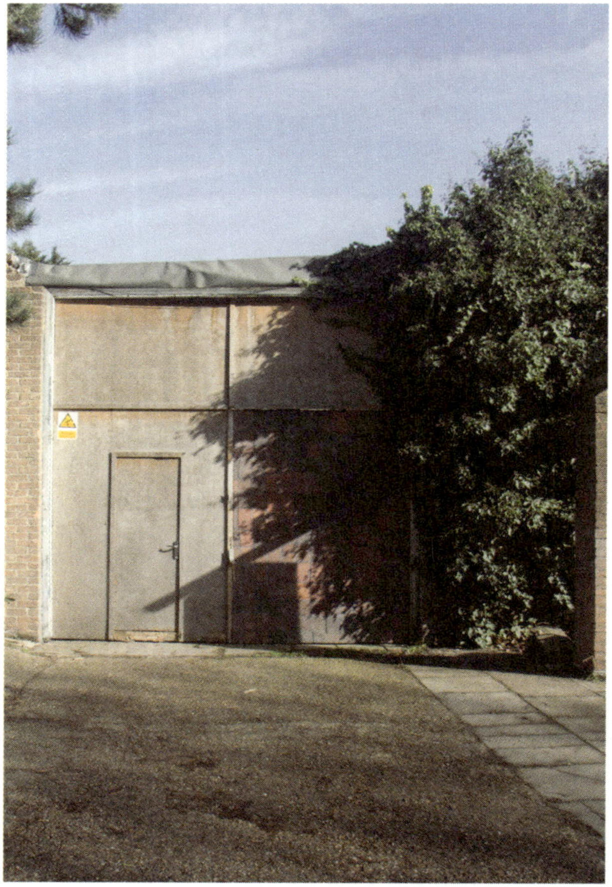

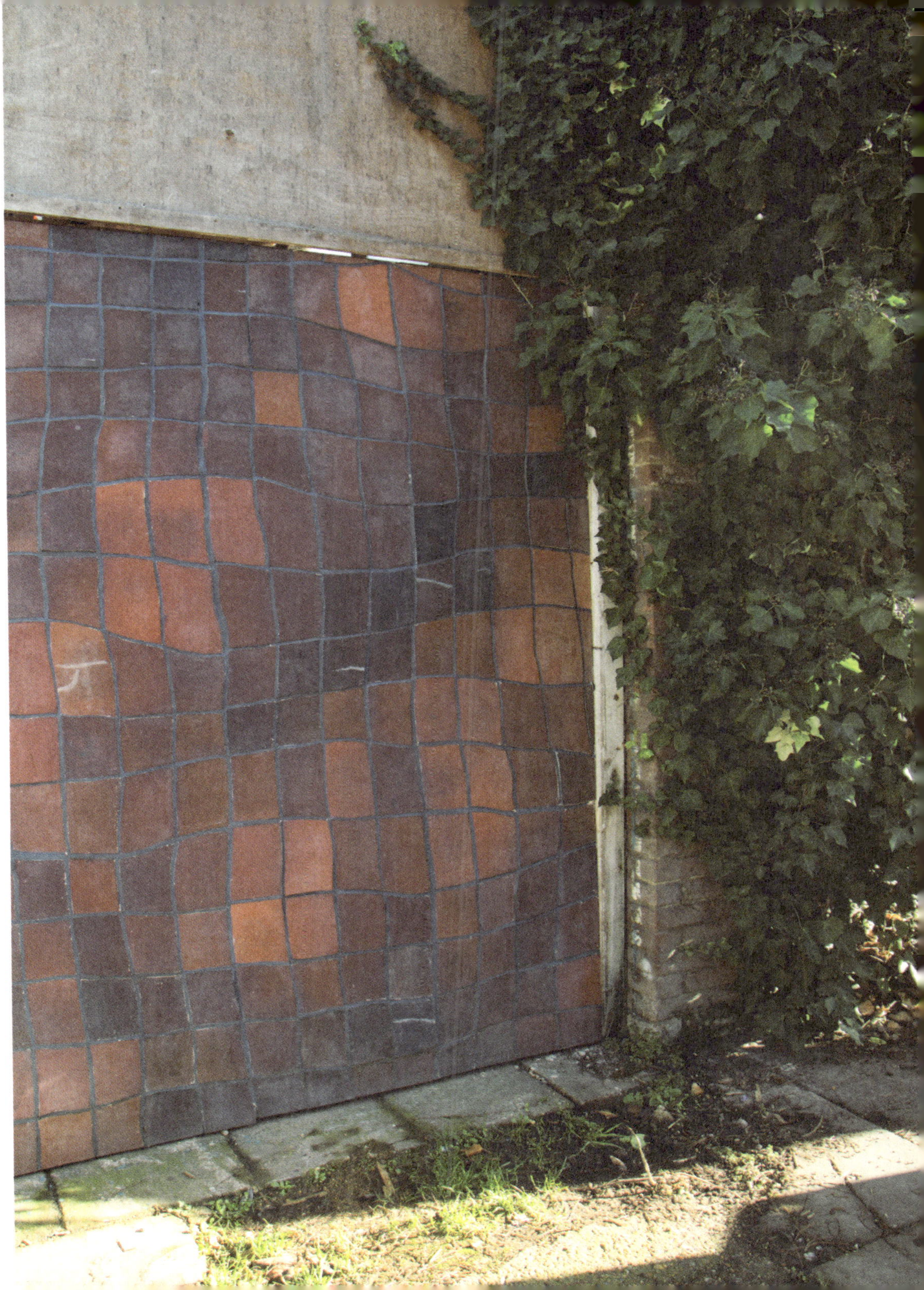

WEEDS — In 2019, artist Tue Greenfort was invited to create a work. His project was inspired by the narrative connected to the eradication of the highly invasive Japanese knotweed from the square, and developed into research on the various types of invasive weeds in the garden. Greenfort then created five large hexagonal reliefs in glazed ceramic. On each, he imprinted the shape of a type of invasive plant collected from the garden, at times mixed with other objects found on-site. The project was initiated by the art agency South into North and supported by the Danish Arts Foundation.

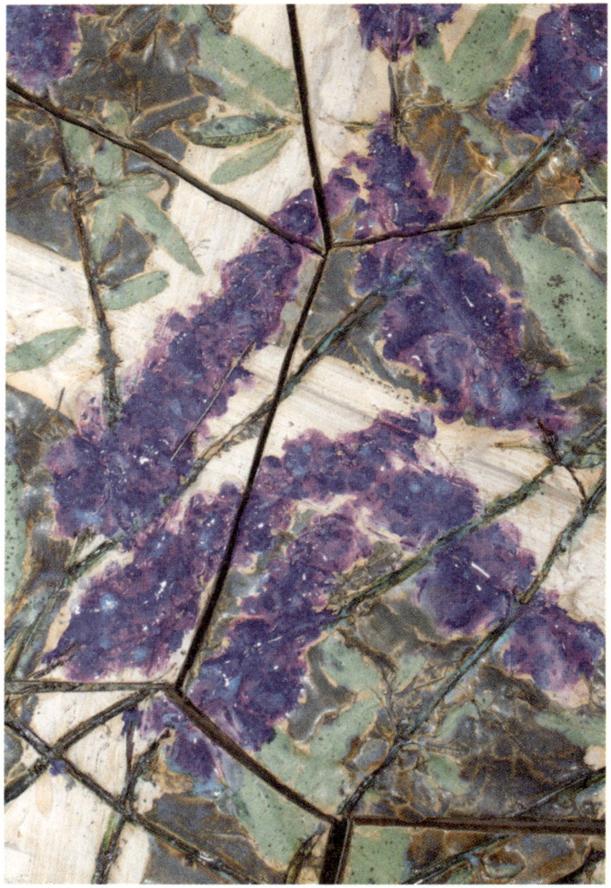

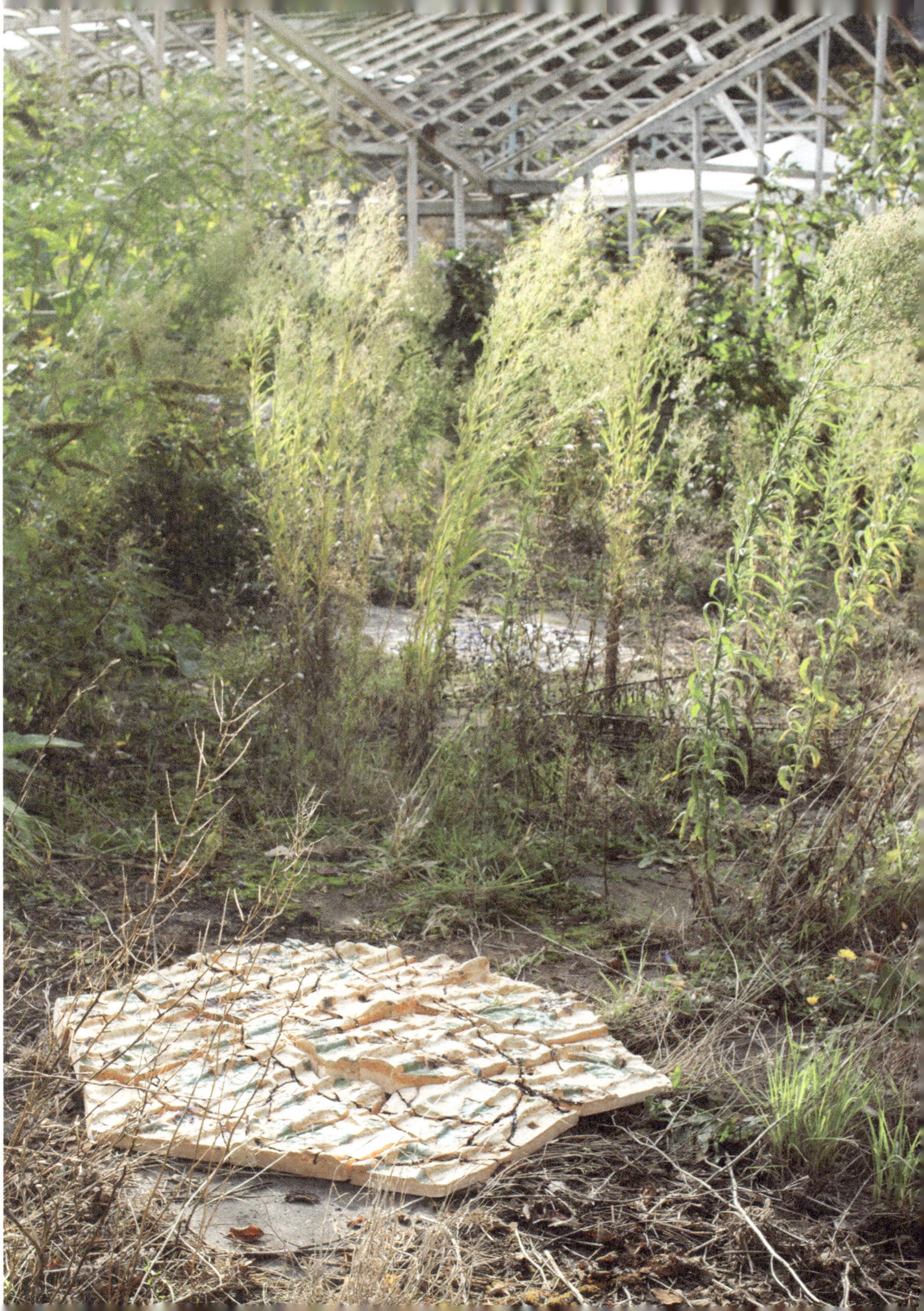

SQUARE MEAL — Rochester Square has organised two editions of a special breakfast called Square Meal, an immersive experience that brings together art, craft and food. Square Meal is an opportunity to get together, eat, experiment and experience our ceramic studio. Exclusive editions of plates, bowls and jugs were made and used to serve refreshments, becoming the stage for an elaborate and playful breakfast experience open to visitors of all ages. This project was created as part of the 2018 Art Licks Weekend and the VIP programme of the 2019 Frieze London art fair.

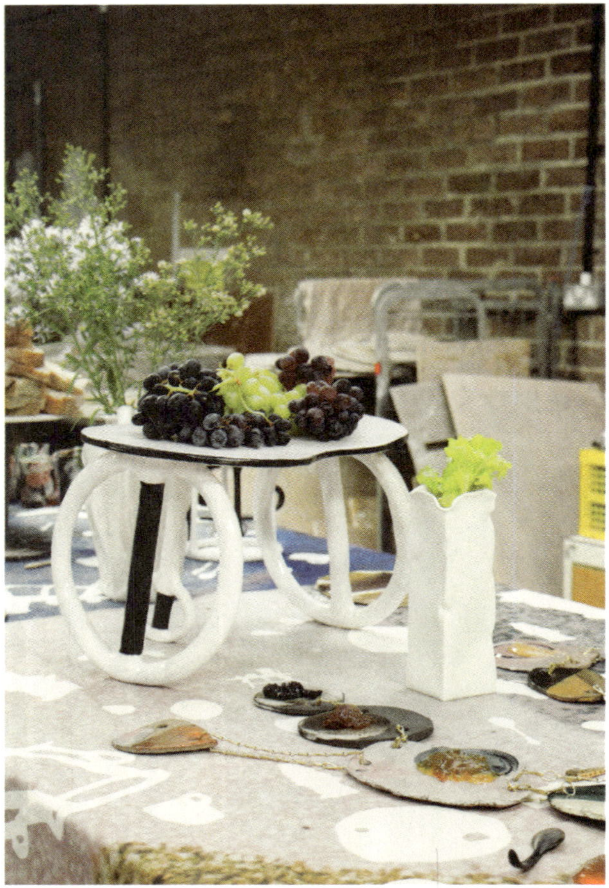

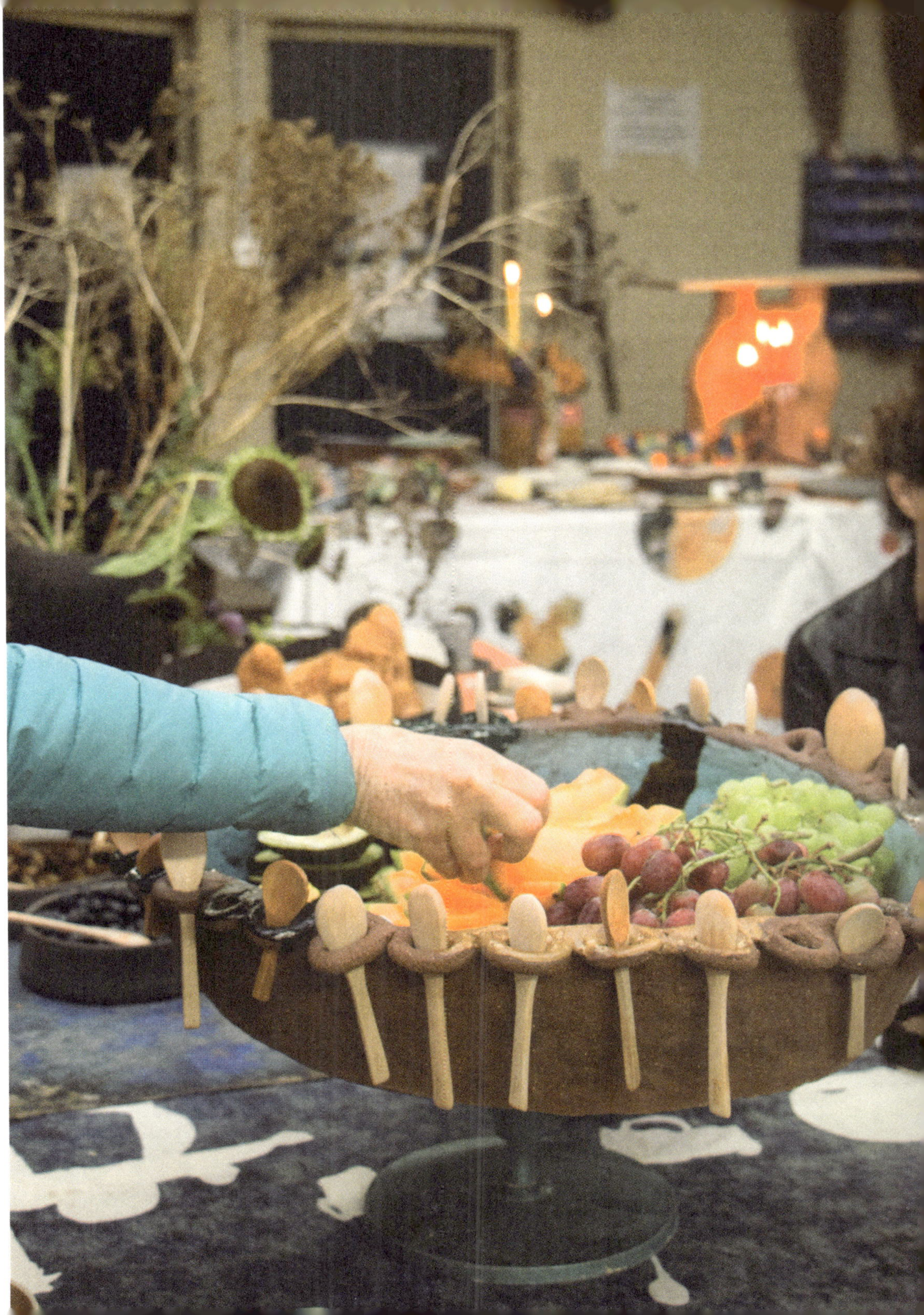

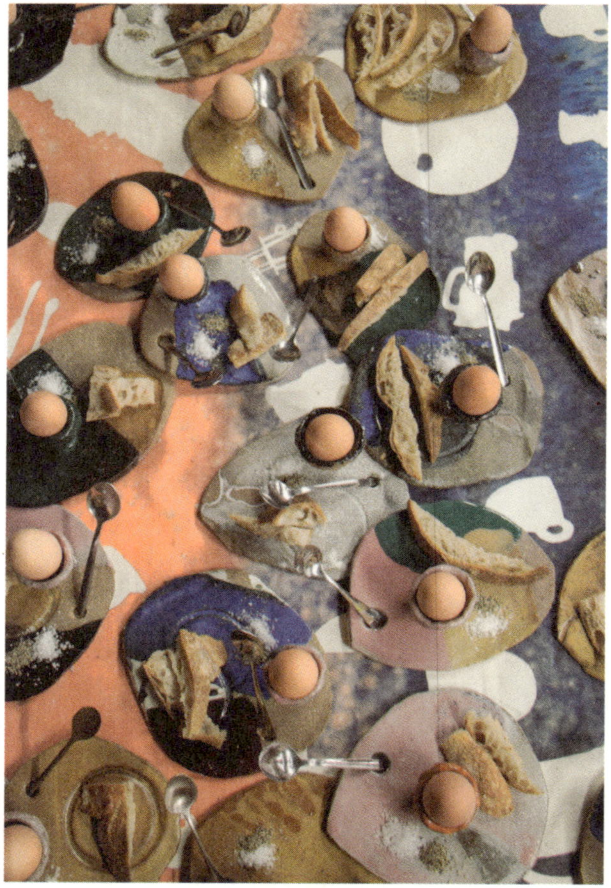

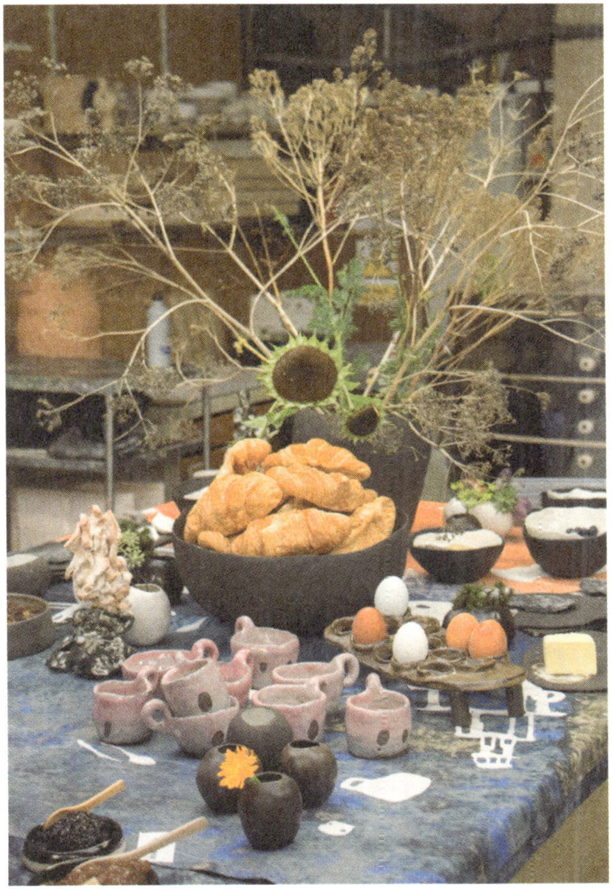

RECIPES — Since 2017, we have been organising a communal dinner on the first Saturday of every other month. A volunteer cooks a meal for those interested in the future of the square, and we share food, stories and ideas for collaborations. There is no rule about what to prepare - usually the meal is a soup or stew in a large pot. The emphasis is on the social aspect of the event, which can host a maximum of forty people. We suggest that after three meals as a guest, the diner becomes the cook. The guests are friends, neighbours and anyone interested in ceramics or food.

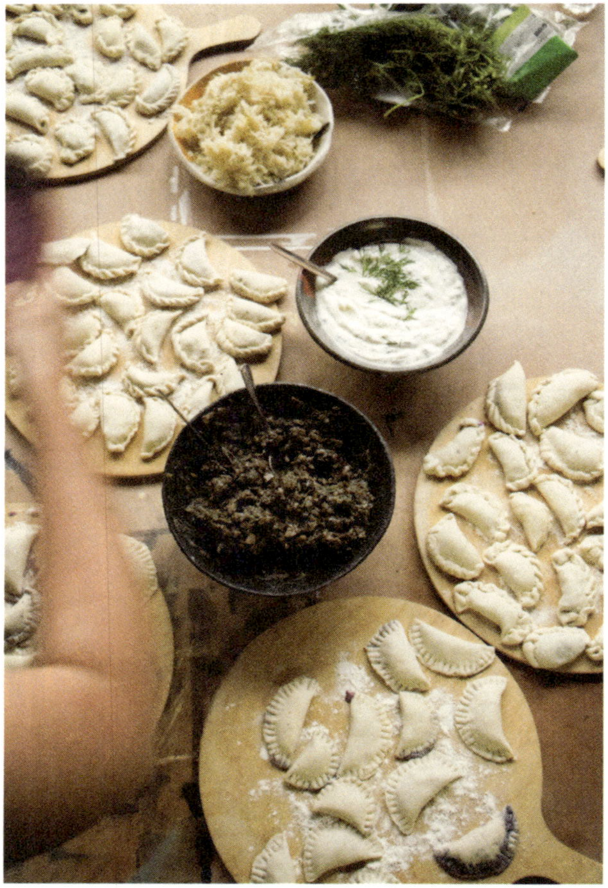

FOOD MAKING — We see the process of clay making and food making as connected and connecting, especially in a convivial sense. Rochester Square is the perfect place to run food workshops, teaching new recipes which often involve kneading, rolling, shaping and other techniques similar to working with clay.

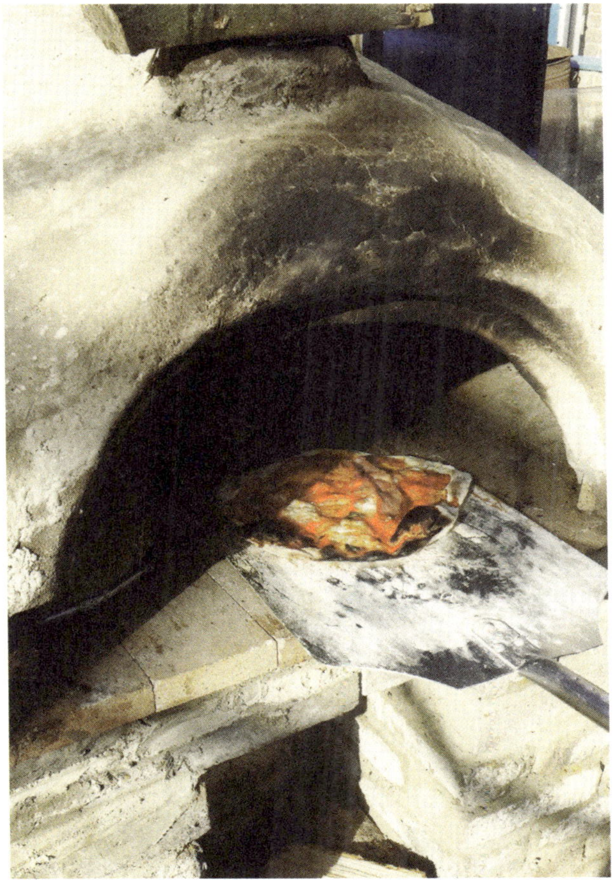

EDUCATION — We value clay as the core material that we walk on and eat from. It is an adaptable, inclusive and nonhierarchical material to work with. We use it daily for some of our most basic activities: in the form of tableware, for children's education or art making, architectural experimentation or crafts therapy. Working with primary schoolchildren has become a major part of our programme and demonstration of the versatility of clay. Special thanks to Kings Cross Academy, Holy Trinity and S. Silas, and Hawley Primary School.

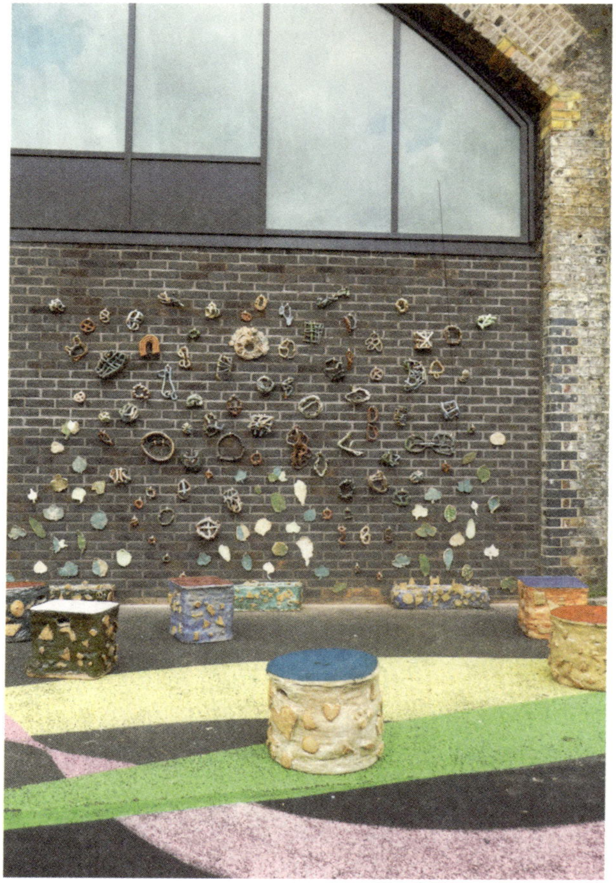

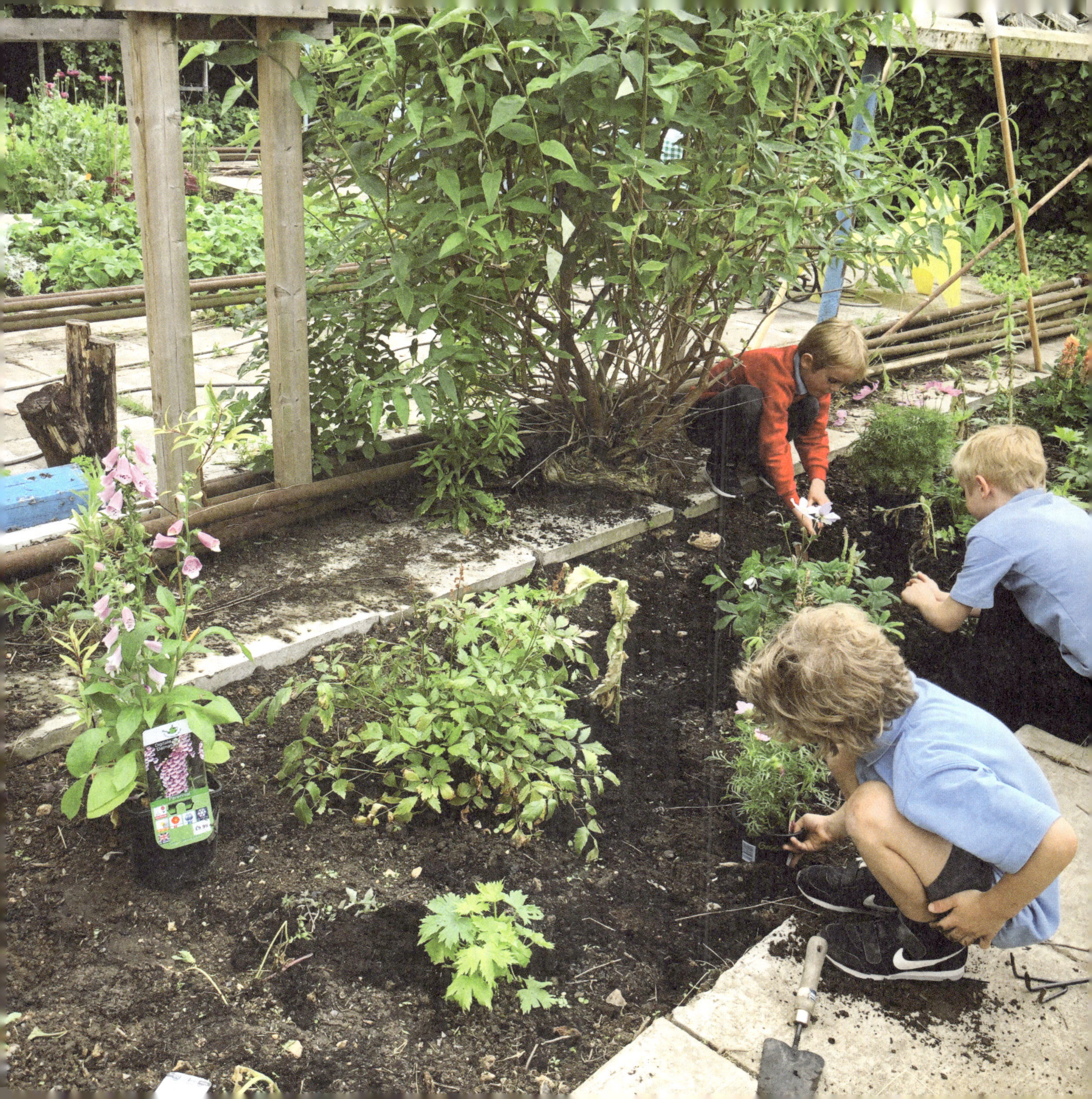

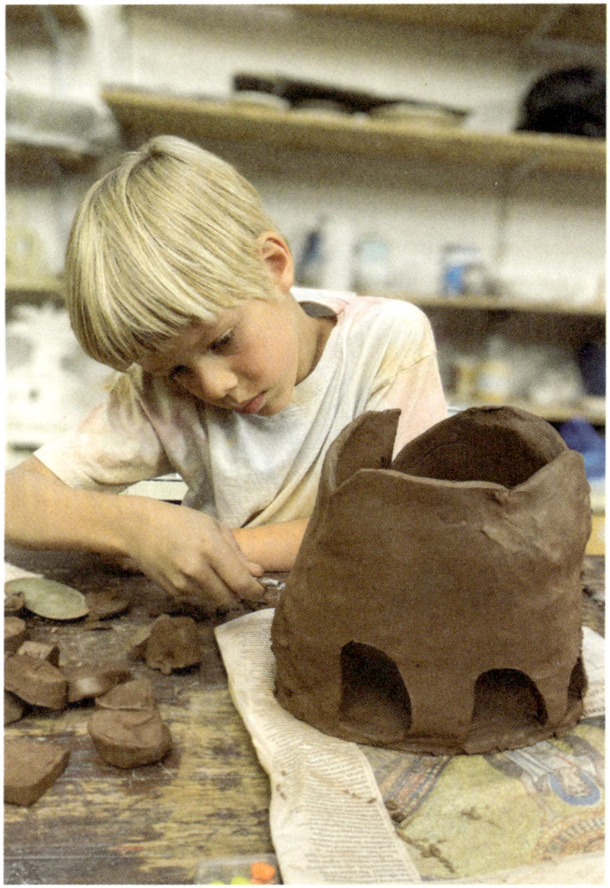

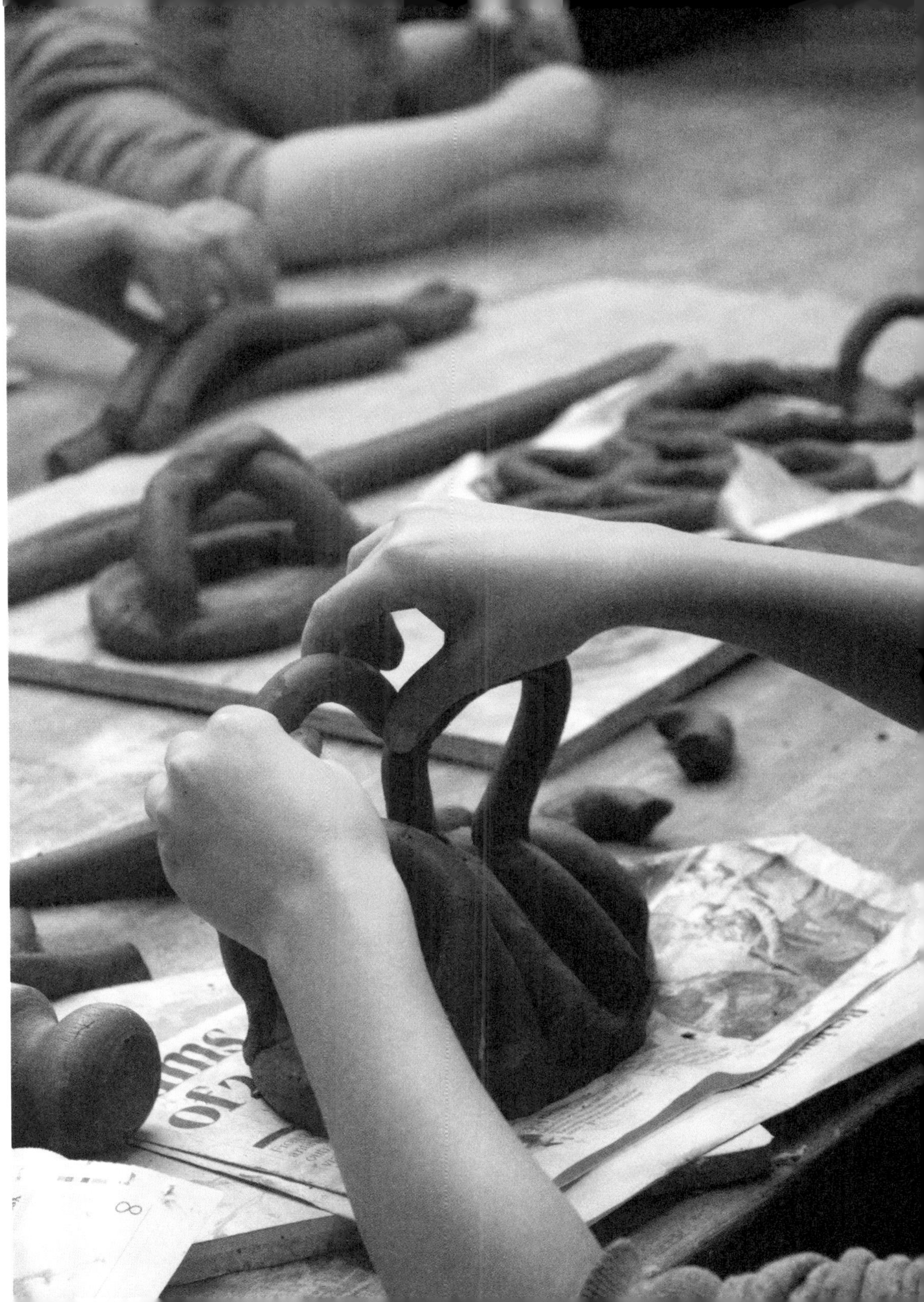

UNIVERSITY OF WESTMINSTER COLLABORATION — In 2018, Rochester Square collaborated with architecture students from the University of Westminster, the local architectural firm Piercy&Company and architect Anthony Boulanger. Learning through making, students used the site as a platform for exploring rituals of eating and drinking. Their interventions and paraphernalia are now part of Rochester Square's temporary sculpture garden.

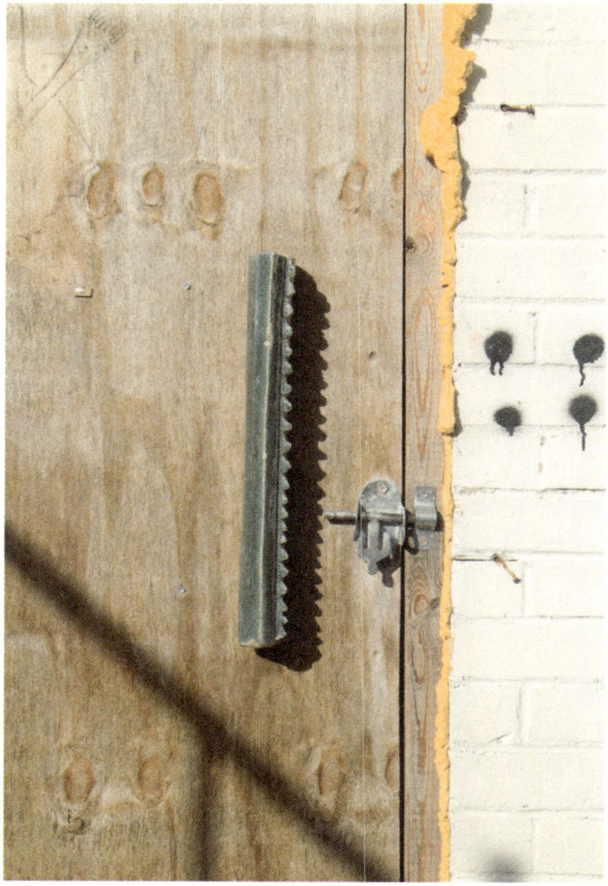

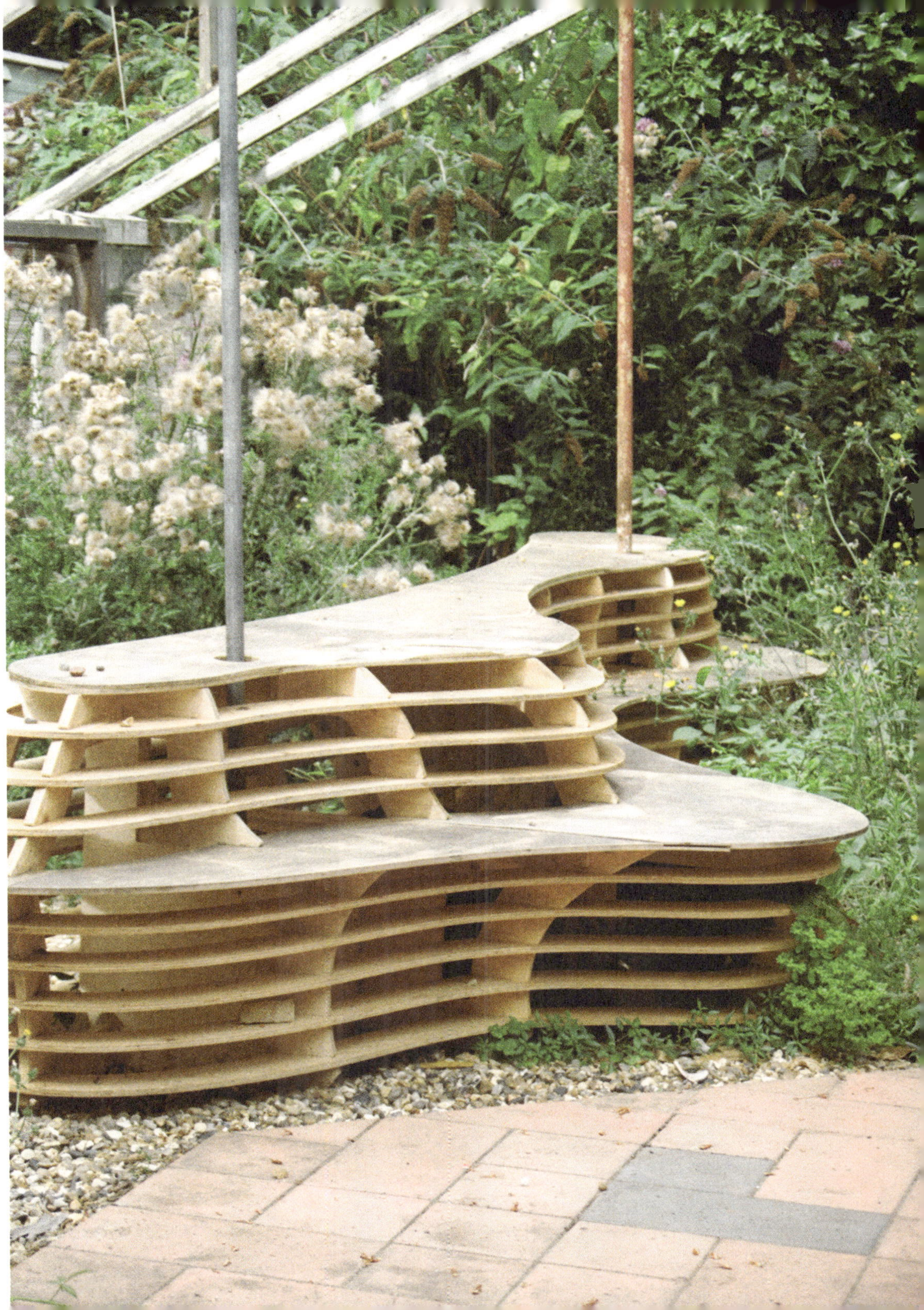

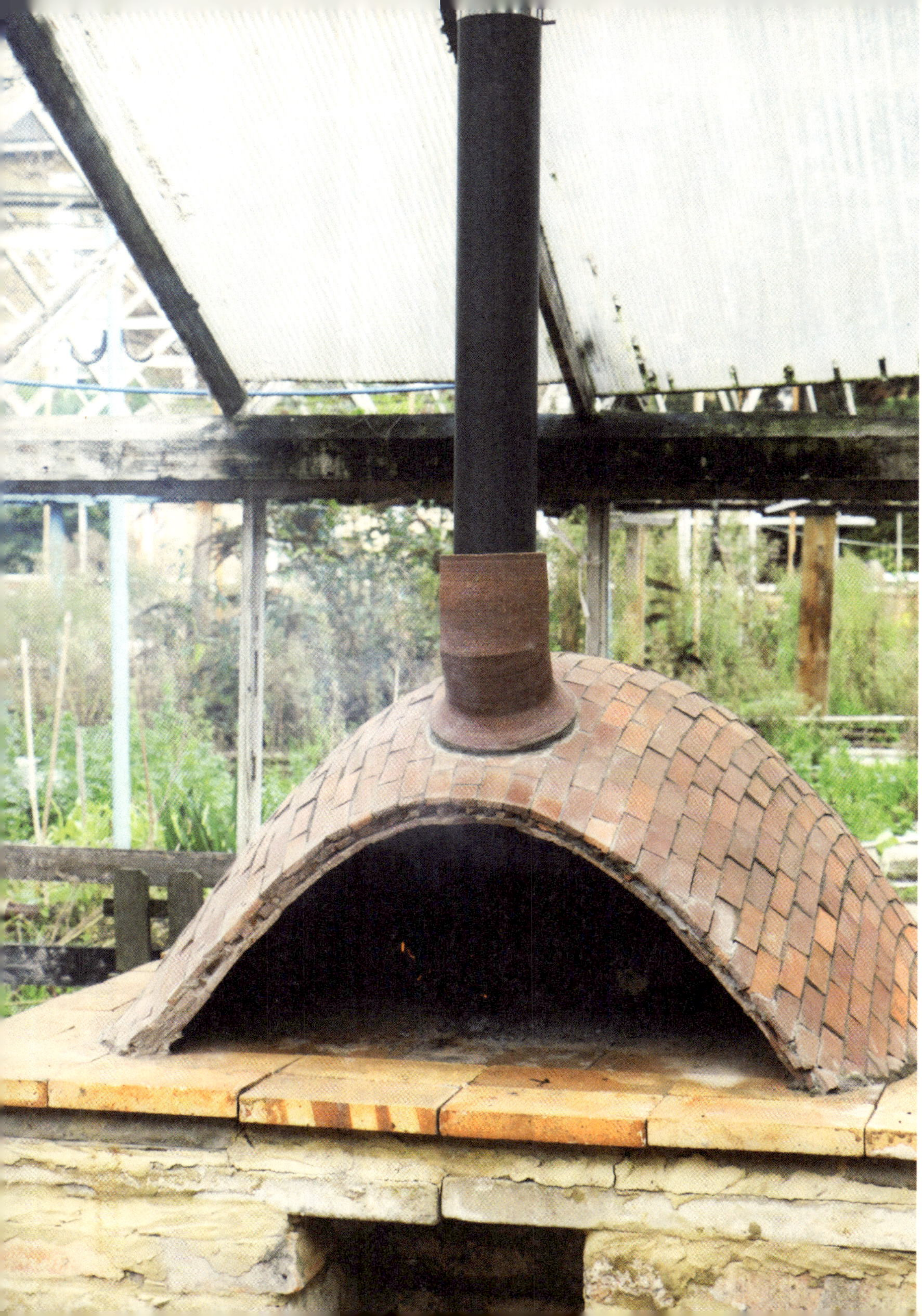

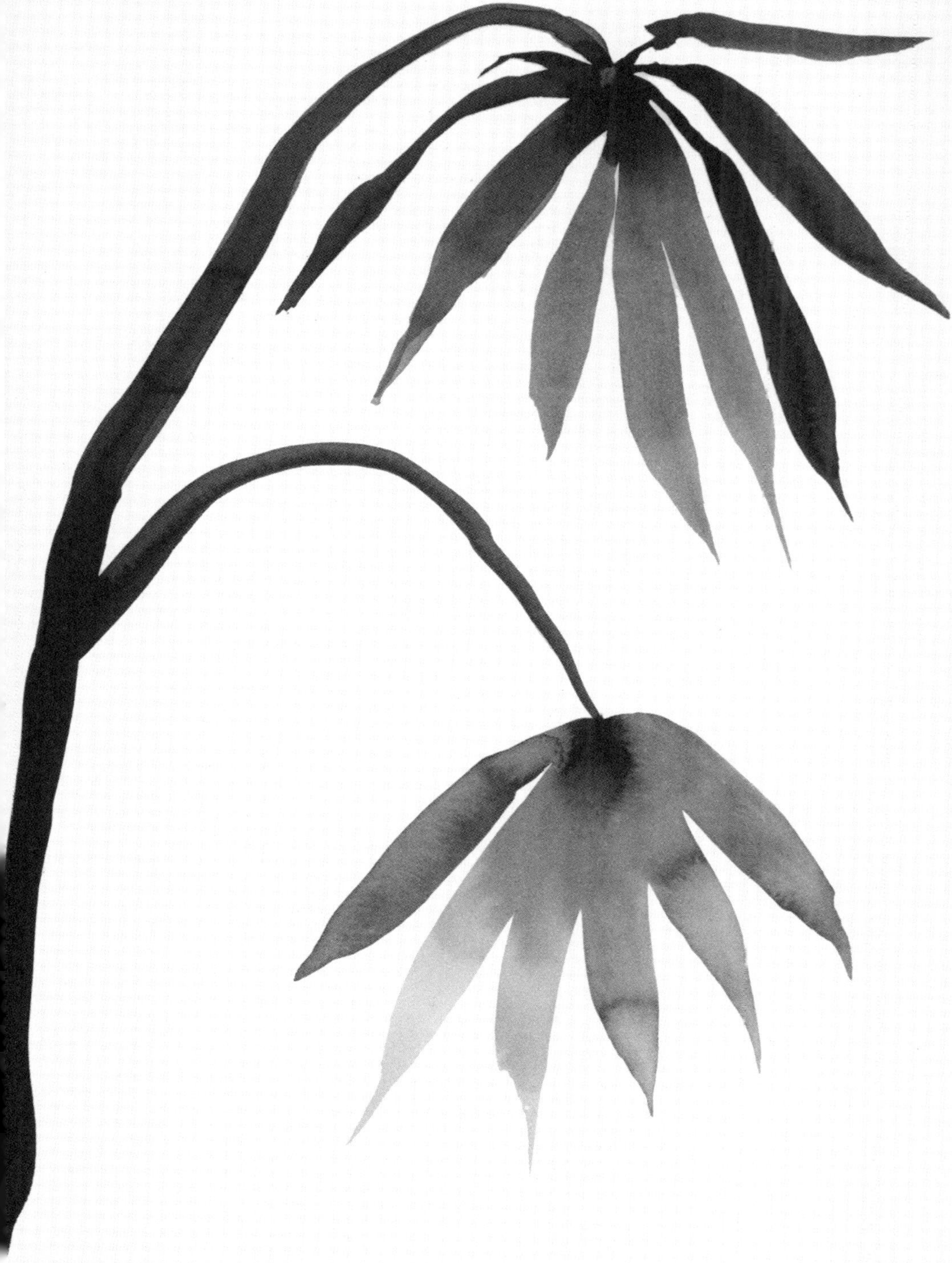

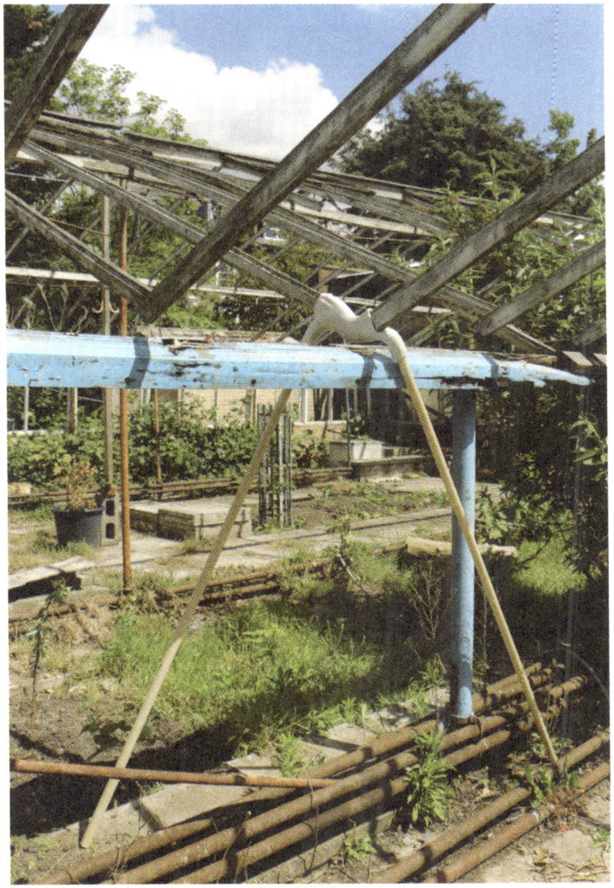

RECREATION DAY — Rochester Square organised its official public launch on 24 and 25 June 2017. We opened the space to the wider community, inviting their involvement in shaping its future and exploring its potential through conversations about a central idea: the use of raw material in situ to respond to ideas of recreation and play. These magical days were possible thanks to the support of many friends, artists, volunteers and local residents and their children.

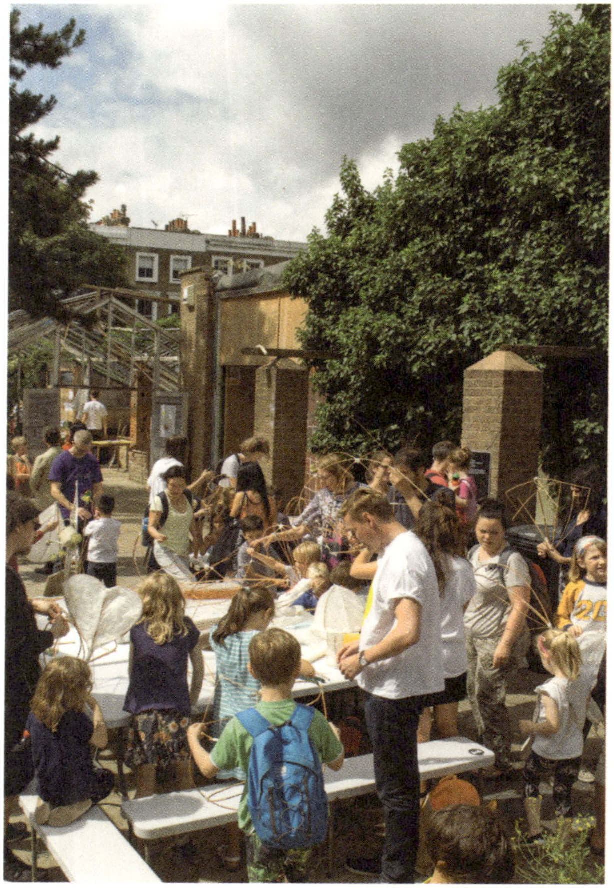

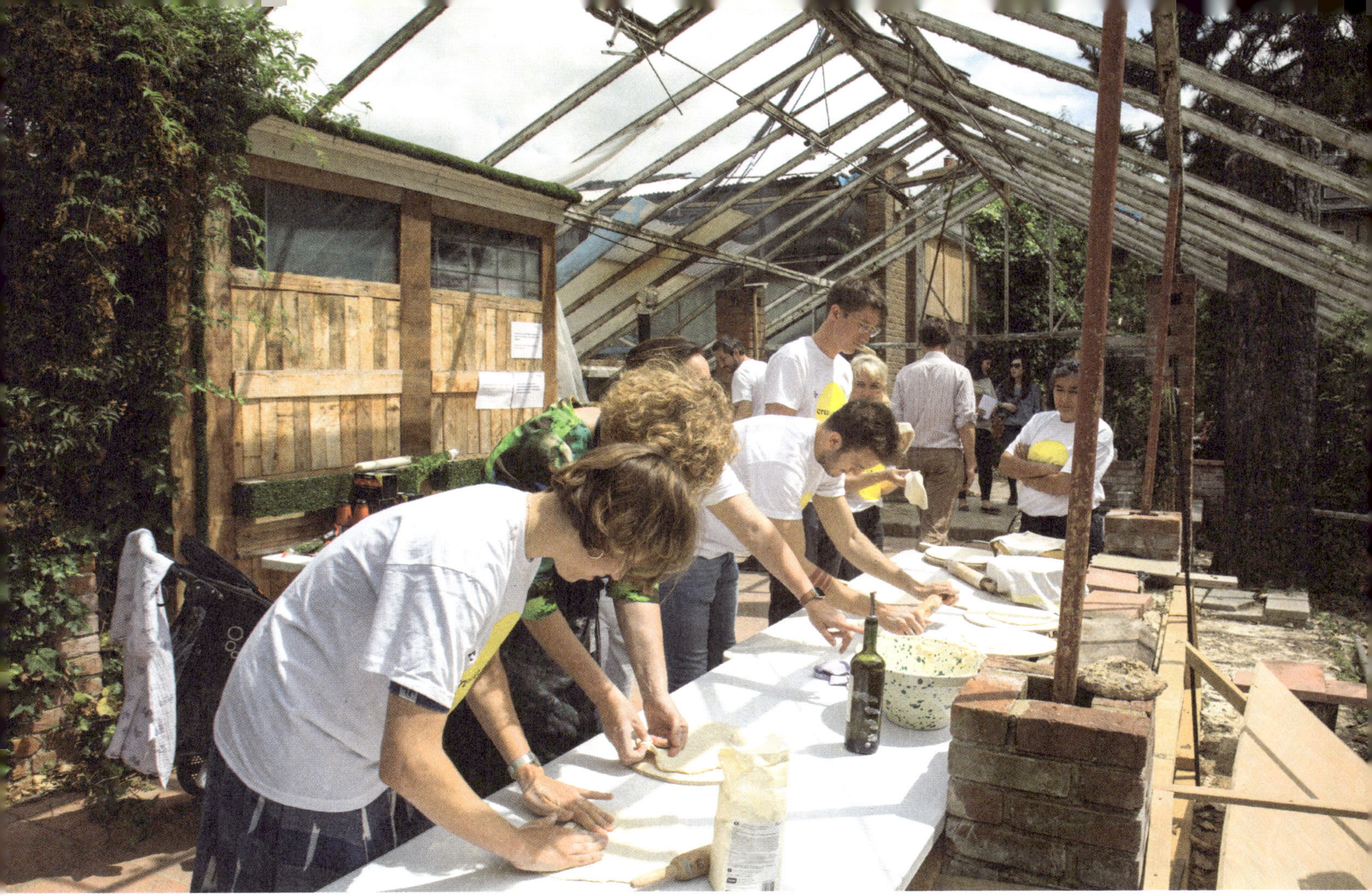

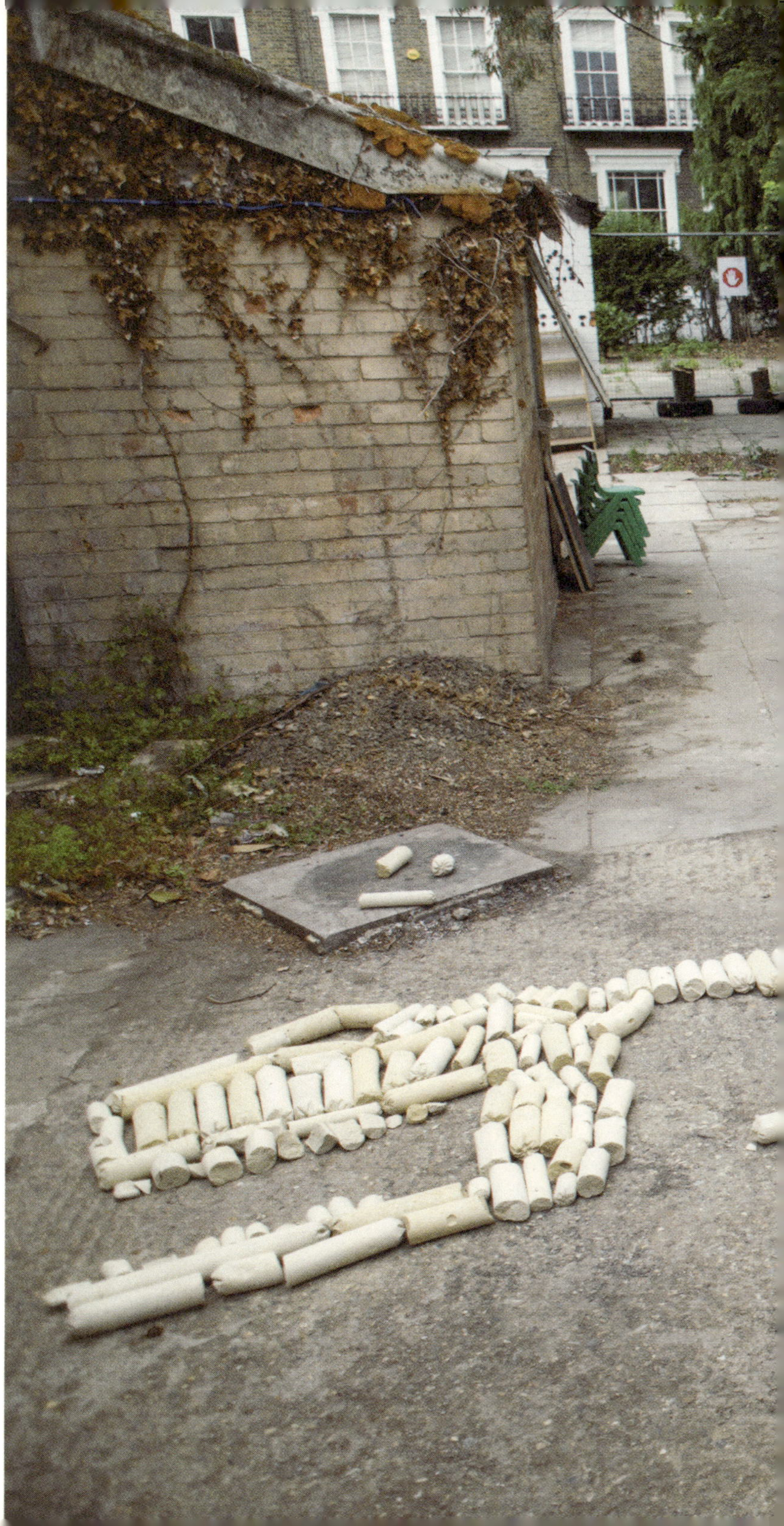

Jamie George, 2017

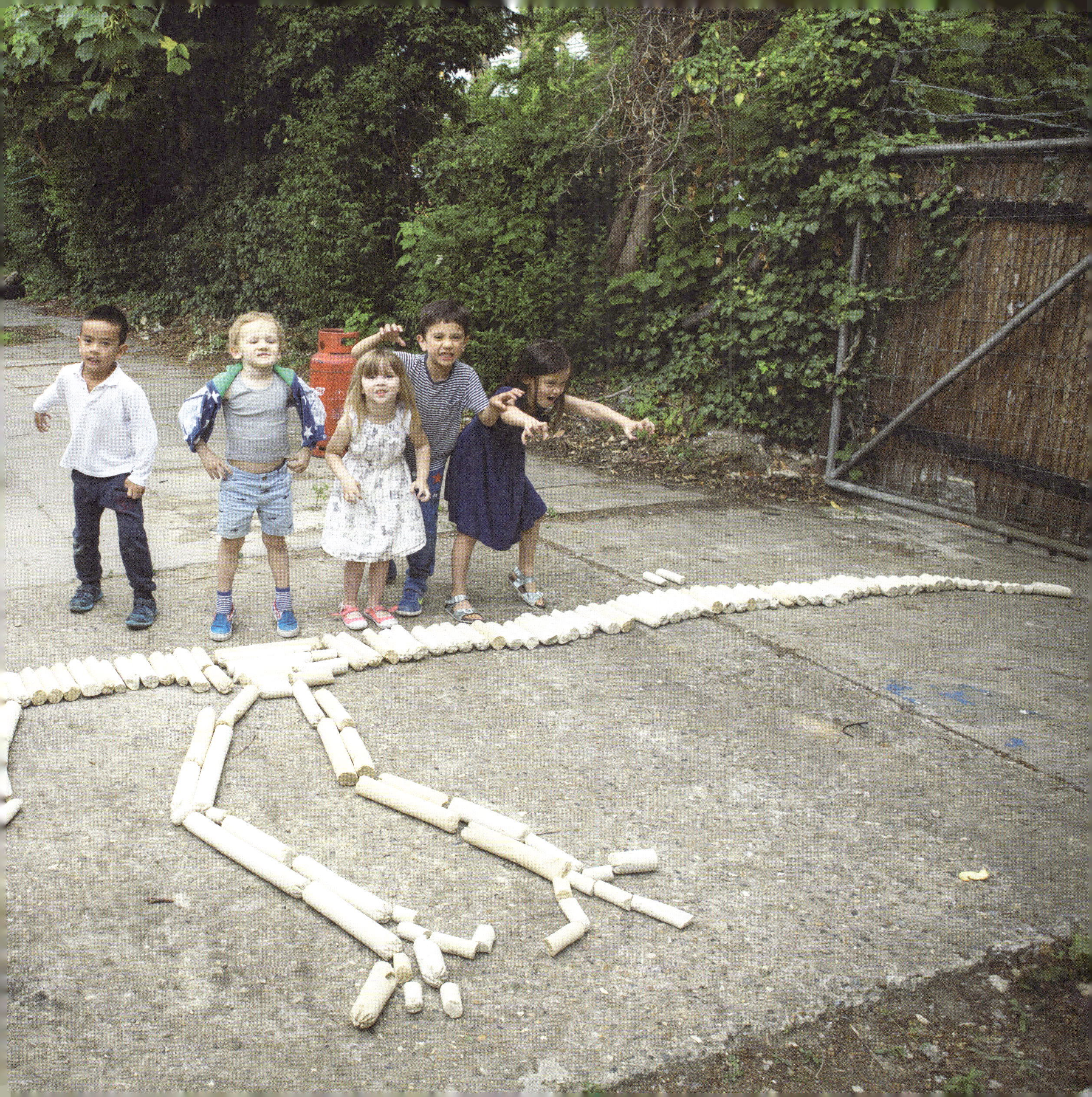

All Things Ceramic
Louise Chignac

Ceramic has one of the richest histories of any medium on the planet, one made of myths, domesticity, technology and art. It was some twenty-six thousand years ago that humans first discovered that clay could be gathered in abundance directly from the ground, and that it could be formed into objects by mixing it with water and using fire. Ever since, ceramic has been part of human lives, and not a single day goes by without us coming into contact with it. Make a list of all clay-related things you can think of. Mine would begin: My much-loved teapot and mugs. The terracotta army. Paris's metro tiles and London's red-brick houses. The plant pots in my garden. My grandmother's Blue Willow china. Ancient Greek urns and Egyptian faience. George Ohr, the mad potter of Biloxi (and his moustache). My children's piggy bank. Ming vases. Pablo Picasso, Lucio Fontana, Lynda Benglis, Ken Price. Rochester Square.

It was on the snowy evening of 3 March 2017 that I attended my first communal dinner at Rochester Square. The atmosphere was friendly, the food and drinks plentiful and the hangover memorable. If I might not precisely remember the conversations and people

I met that night, what I do remember is the ceramics, the plates especially. As I arrived at Rochester Square that evening, Francesca informed me rather nervously that the plates were not ready *yet* because they were too *hot*. She wasn't talking dishwasher-hot, she was talking kiln-hot. The idea of eating off a freshly baked plate left me flabbergasted. I realised that, despite using ceramic plates for three meals a day, I had never really looked at them as being objects made from the soil – from minerals, plants, animals, from life. As soon as the plates had cooled down enough for us to enjoy our *minestrone alla genovese*, the simple experience of eating felt new to me. More than this, it felt like magic, with Francesca as the magician.

Ever since that evening, I have never missed a communal dinner at Rochester Square, and I have developed an active interest in the social histories of plates, cups, bowls and pitchers that we use every day. I see clay everywhere, from ceramic tiles on bathroom walls and kitchen splashbacks to the bricks, mortar, cement and concrete that make the houses where we live and the buildings where we work. It never fails to fascinate me that, worldwide, our cities, tableware and even the most advanced technology that sends us into space are made of the same matter, and that this very matter comes from right under our feet. Even our most famous myths of creation centre on ceramic. Think of Prometheus who shaped man out of mud while Athena breathed life into his clay figure; of the god Khnum who created human children from clay before placing them into their mother's womb; and of Enki, the Sumerian god of water, knowledge and crafts, who formed humankind out of clay and blood. Ceramic's association with creation extends to extraordinary artwork. The first evidence of human-made ceramics dates back to at least 24000 BCE, long before the wheel, the kiln, porcelain plates, glazed pitchers and my grandmother's Blue Willow china. It is an object of worship, a statuette known as the Venus of Dolní Věstonice. Found along with hundreds of broken clay animal figurines in a cave in what is now the Czech Republic, these objects and their function seem to hint at an element of the ritualistic and magical. As objects, they were brought forth from the earth, sculpted, only to be broken and cast back into the very place of their origin.

Clay's ubiquity, accessibility and malleable nature have allowed it to be one of the few materials of the ancient world that escaped any hierarchical classification, having never been reserved for a unique function. The material happily lends itself to all functions – plate, bowl, religious vessel or magical figurine – bridging the gap between the rich and the poor, high and low culture, design and utility. Ceramic as a medium constantly flitters between art and craft; it generously straddles both simultaneously and without discrimination. Clay has no time for aesthetic politics or the musings of disgruntled critics. It will be whatever it *needs* to be.

Contrary to popular thought, most inventions were not made to meet a specific need or desire at a specific time or place. The application or need of a product was often developed later on to supplement the invention itself. But with clay and ceramics, it truly is the other way around: the need for such a material was there long before the discovery itself. Our ancestors who first entered caves to create what is now known as the earliest form of art had to find stones with a hollow depression in order to be able to hold the fuel and wick so they could light their way into the dark tunnels. How much simpler it would have been to make what is essentially a bowl of any size you wish out of clay! At the same time, those very same people were laboriously carving human and animal figurines out of bone or wood. Take the famous Lion-Man ivory sculpture in Germany. It is estimated to have taken an expert artist around four hundred hours to create, a truly time-consuming task; made of clay, it would have only taken a few. Having helped us shape our lives and fulfil our dreams and fantasies, clay is an irreducible material that continues to connect us to earth, to our bodies and history as human beings.

Is that what ceramic is about? Connections? Creating a bridge between our most basic needs, such as eating, drinking and socialising, and our most refined activities, such as art, technology and rituals? Maybe it is the medium that binds it all, that connects us to our Neolithic ancestors and the universe. Clay offers sensory impact and associations that are singular, perhaps even fundamental. Childhood memories of manipulating Plasticine, Play-Doh or clay lead to an association of clay with 'play' and something instinctive, innately human, visceral. It connects to our most tactile experiences, therefore taking us away from that uncomfortable feeling that art should be elitist or conceptual. As participatory and collaborative practices across the arts grow, so does the demand towards social exchange and conversation, and this is where Rochester Square is pertinent. It is both a studio and a workshop that offers facilities such as kilns and a sharing of skills that few British art schools now teach, as well as a strong sense of community that has become vital to many of its users and neighbours.

Just like clay, Rochester Square is about connections, or rather connecting – people, food and earth all form part of an art project that is larger than life. It takes the form of a place to gather and share, to create and experiment. Handling clay is only the start of the process; it is not an easy material to manipulate well, it is mutable but also willing to change and adapt to the hands that form it. It is so crudely analogue, it somehow goes against the digital world we live in. Above all, it brings us down to size and reminds us of what we are, as human beings. Precarious by nature, it bears life and accompanies ours on a daily basis.

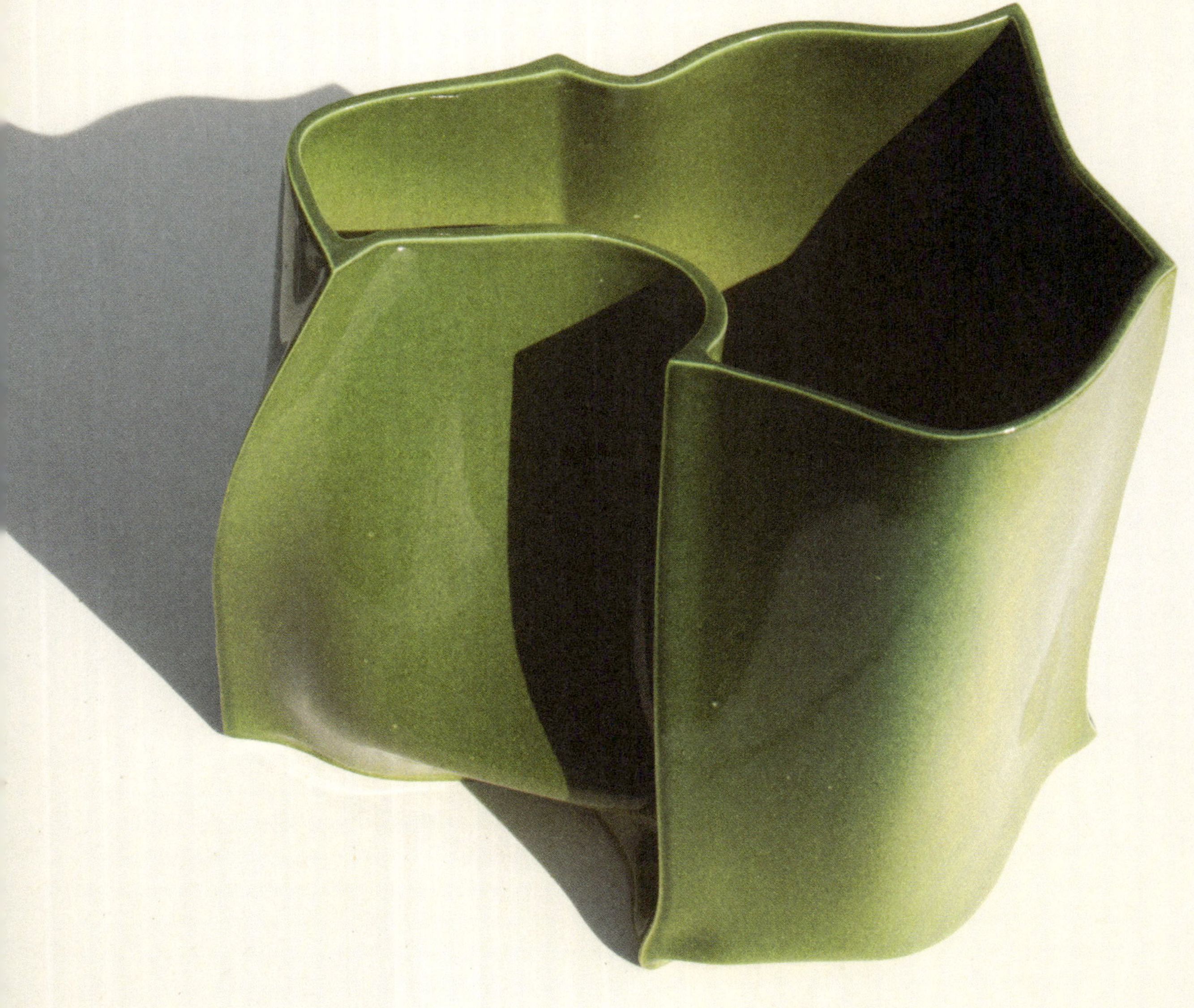

Philipp Schenk-Mischke, 2019

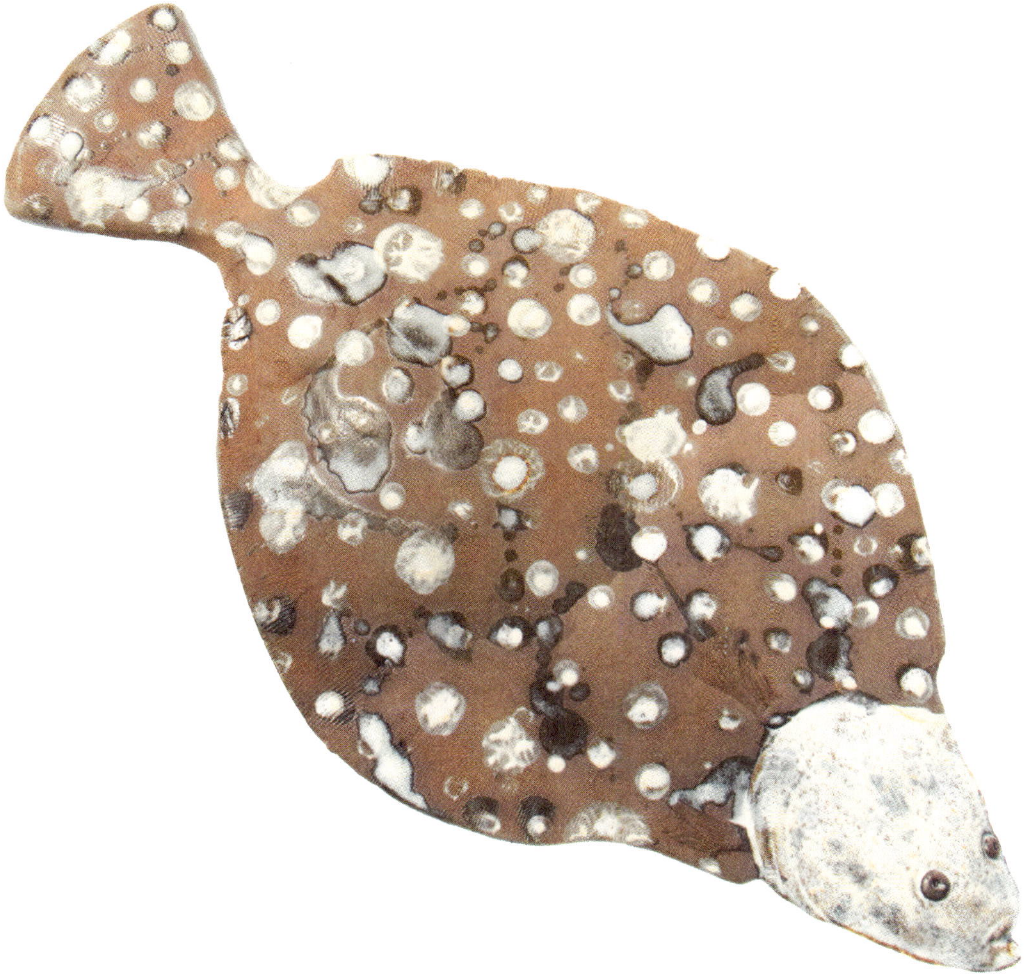

Sarah Staton, 2020

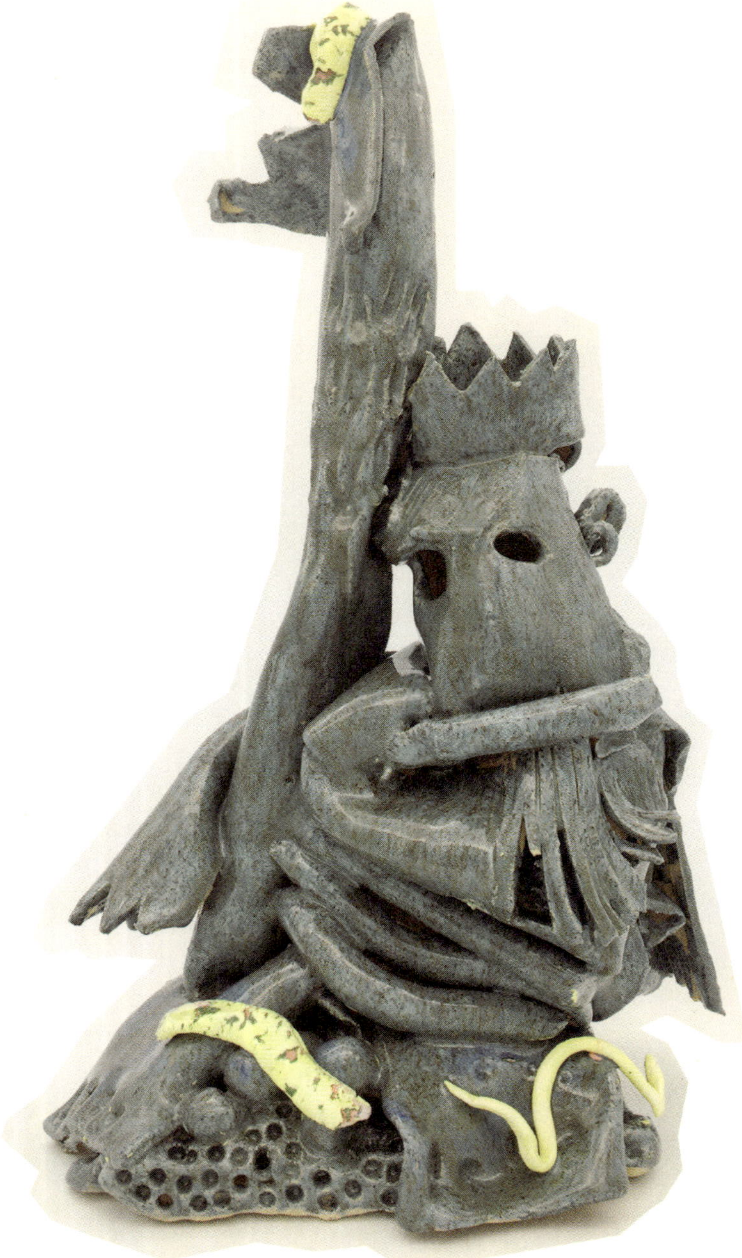

Paulina Michnowska, 2020

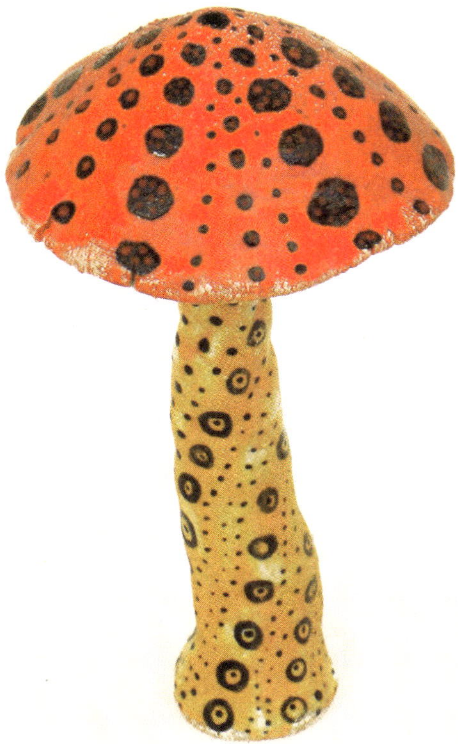

Kiramics, 2018

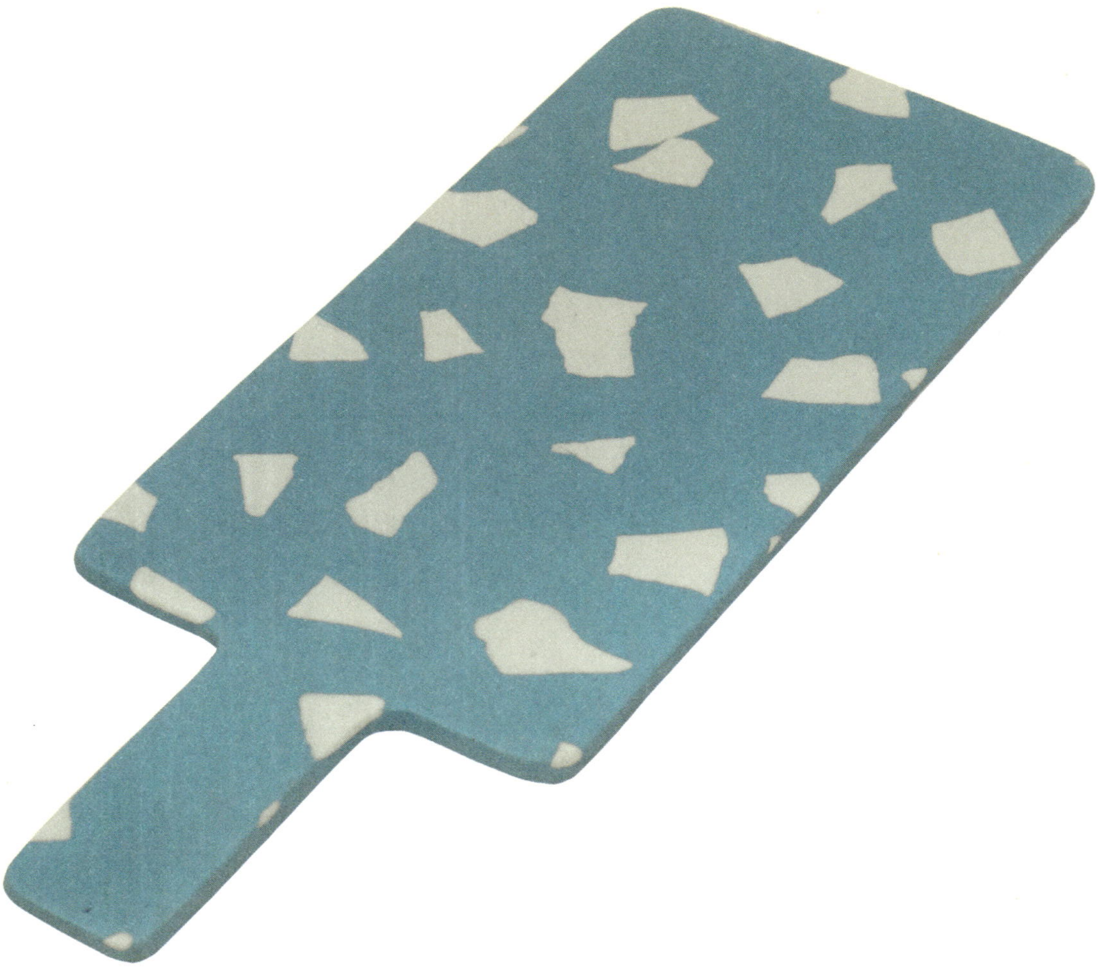

Sevak Zargarian, 2018

Francesca Anfossi is a multidisciplinary artist and co-founder of Rochester Square. Her work most often takes the form of ceramics, workshops, cooking classes or communal events, and offers the participants opportunities to learn new skills and form new social bonds. She recently contributed to the project SupaStore Southside at South London Gallery (2021) and was a finalist for the 2020 Whitegold International Ceramic Prize.

Francesca Astesani is an independent curator, writer and educator based in Copenhagen. She is a regular contributor to *Kunstkritikk* and *Artforum* and co-director and co-founder of the curatorial agency South into North, which specialises in contemporary art commissions. She has run projects in collaboration with institutions including the Tate Modern, Pirelli HangarBicocca, Fondazione Prada, the New Museum and Haus der Kunst, and artists such as Cally Spooner, Philippe Parreno, Kapwani Kiwanga, Roman Signer and Pipilotti Rist.

Louise Chignac is co-founder and director of Canopy Collections. She has collaborated with leading art collections and galleries worldwide, such as Cranford Collections (London), Kadist Art Foundation (Paris) and Ordovas (London and New York), and contributed to the first edition of the Art Night Festival in London. As a curator, she has exhibited the work of Francis Alÿs, Francesca Anfossi, Susan Hiller, Pierre Huyghe, Derek Jarman, Bruno Ollé, Laure Prouvost, Dan Rees and Ulay.

Polly Farquharson is a London-based artist and author. Her work has appeared in the magazines *World of Interiors*, *Blueprint* and *Casa Vogue*, and she wrote the children's book *The Green Line* (Frances Lincoln, 2011).

Marta Fernàndez is a London-based photographer and former studio manager at Rochester Square. Her photographic work has been featured in "Tallers Oberts," A-FAD, Montoya, Barcelona (2018); Food, Design & Femininity Festival, Barcelona (2017); and "Young Blood," Shed Gallery, Barcelona (2014).

Chris Fite-Wassilak is a writer, critic and former cheesemonger based in London. He is a contributing editor for *ArtReview* and a regular contributor to *Art Agenda*, *Camera Austria* and *frieze*. His books include *The Artist in Time* (Herbert Press, 2020) and *Ha-Ha Crystal* (Copy Press, 2016), and his writing appears in *Politics of Food* (Sternberg Press, 2019) and *Curating Research* (Open Editions, 2014).

Emily King is a London-based writer and curator specialising in design. Recent projects include curating the Beazley Designs of the Year 2020 exhibition for London's Design Museum and writing an extended profile of Rem Koolhaas for *Fantastic Man* (Spring/Summer 2020). She is curating an exhibition on the theme of ornament that will open at the Drawing Center, New York, in June 2022. Emily writes a regular column for *MacGuffin*.

This project and book could never have been created without the input and help of many.

I would like to thank all the former and current members, neighbours and 'passers-through' of Rochester Square for trusting and supporting us from the beginning, and for continually filling and refilling the project and space with positive energy. Since taking on the project in 2016, our efforts to revive Rochester Square and manage the day-to-day of the space have been a collaboration with many, especially artists and friends Giulia Astesani, Maria Gibert, Nam Tran, Gerald Mak, Marta Fernàndez, Sam Belinfante, Sarah Kate Wilson, Sevak Zargarian, Matteo Ricordo, Alessandro Gugel, Toby O'Connor, the late and loved Leviathen Hendricks, Danielle Goulé and Penny Clayden.

Our hearts and stomachs are grateful to those who cooked communal dinners with generosity and enthusiasm: Frank Hannon, Fanny Singer, Filipa Ramos, Paulina Michnowska, Hattie Spires, Kitty Travers, Anna Tobias, Nissa Nishikawa, Sam Belinfante, Leviathen Hendricks, George Moustakas, Lucy Steggals, Gerald Mak, Yoojin Lee, Marta Fernàndez, Jordi Canals, Raquel Sales, Ambra Medda, Edward Barber, Milan Tarascas and Ellie Wang. Even those who said they 'couldn't cook' always managed to make a delicious and memorable meal for thirty to forty people.

A lot of effort went into the preparation of each dinner, and a special thanks goes to all the volunteers as well as Marta Fernàndez and Maria Gibert for always being there from before the first table was set until the last glass was collected from the garden and the lights switched off.

In bringing this book together, I am indebted to the team at A Practice for Everyday Life for their precise, dynamic design that brings together clay, food and garden. Thanks to Emily King, Francesca Astesani, Chris Fite-Wassilak and Louise Chignac for their inspiring texts; Polly Farquharson for the beautiful illustrations of the plants she grew in the garden; Marta Fernàndez for the photographs, assemblage of background material and persuasion to make the book in the first place; and Emily King, Antony Gormley and South into North for their precious advice and support.

— Francesca Anfossi

From the Pot to the Earth at Rochester Square
Edited by Francesca Anfossi

Published by Sternberg Press

Copyediting: Max Bach
Design: A Practice for Everyday Life
Printing: Tallinn Book Printers, Estonia
Photography: Marta Fernàndez
Illustrations: Polly Farquharson

ISBN 978-3-95679-624-1

Distributed by The MIT Press, Art Data, and Les presses du réel

Sternberg Press
71–75 Shelton Street
London WC2H 9JQ
sternberg-press.com